Bulbs
for all climates

Bulbs are one of nature's most intriguing creations – ready-made flowers squeezed into a convenient package. They grow, bloom and die back in a matter of months and, just when you've forgotten them, they reappear to do it all over again, only bigger and better than before. To avoid disappointment, it is important that you choose the right bulbs for your climate and that's where this book can really help. It gives details on the climatic needs of more than 150 varieties, along with all the other information you'll need to grow them successfully. For easy reference, we have given all plant dimensions and planting depths in metric and imperial measurements, rounded off to the nearest whole number.

GARDENING EDITOR

❖ ❖ ❖

The World of Bulbs

NATURE'S OWN, READY TO BLOOM PACKAGES

There are more types of bulbs available, many of which produce flowers of the utmost charm and beauty, than most gardeners realise. In this book, we introduce you to some of the most exciting of these strangers.

Below: Possibly the world's most popular bulb, hybrid tulips signify spring practically everywhere. But did you know that there are many beautiful species as well? We show you several on page 112.

No matter where you live, the range of bulbs that you can easily grow is probably wider and more interesting than you realise. And, if you are prepared to go to some trouble to meet their specific needs, your choice will be even bigger.

Bulbs are found in most climate regions and on every continent. And, while it is true that some climates are much more suitable for bulbs than others, there are few places where bulb growing is out of the question.

Above: Who would guess that this is a daffodil? 'Rip van Winkle' is just one of many unusually shaped or coloured hybrid daffodils available. Turn to page 96 for information on daffodils.

Most bulb books are written from a cold or cool-climate gardener's viewpoint. Naturally, they concentrate on cold-climate bulbs, but these bulbs are only part of the picture. For every species that grows in a cool or cold climate, there is another that is native to a warmer region. Despite their surprising beauty, warm-climate bulbs are often little known, even in their homelands. We have

included several such bulbs in the hope of broadening their appeal. Of course, these are best suited to areas where frosts are light or unknown, but most bulbs can also be grown in cooler areas – outside in summer or in pots in the greenhouses and conservatories that are popular features of gardens in the northern hemisphere.

As well as these curious warm-climate species, you'll find fascinating examples of many cold-climate bulbs. Some of these are well known, others may surprise and delight you with their beauty and novelty. Where a genus is well known, we have tried to show you examples of the more unusual species or hybrids that are available.

Above: In good conditions, some bulbs multiply so fast that you can soon have an impressive massed display. Here, thousands of bluebells bloom together, creating a meadow of colour. Find out about Hyacinthoides on page 84.

This book is divided into three sections. The introductory chapters outline the various climates from which bulbs come and how to choose the most suitable species for your garden. We offer advice on how and where to plant them, and how to maintain and propagate them. We also help you to identify and control pests and diseases that may strike.

Above: More like a sea creature than a flower, South Africa's Ferraria is one of the bulb world's oddities. You'll discover how to grow this exotic-looking species on page 76.

The pictorial section follows. It contains detailed information on individual bulbs and about 160 species are illustrated in colour.

In the middle of the book you'll find a calendar of the bulb grower's year. Here, for each month of each season, we list the most important tasks you should undertake to keep your bulbs in top condition. There is also a flowering calendar so you know what to expect and when.

Beautiful Bulbs

BULBS, CORMS, TUBERS AND RHIZOMES

What is it about bulbs that keeps them so close to the hearts of gardeners? As a group, they rival roses in numbers sold, are far more popular than orchids, and much more keenly sought than annuals.

Perhaps it's because some are seen as symbols of spring, gorgeous and colourful heralds of the warmer, easier days to come. Or maybe it's because success is so easy; flowering is a virtual certainty, in the first year at least. Then again, it may be the blooms themselves that attract us – bulbs do produce some of the world's loveliest flowers. Whatever the reason, the continued popularity of bulbs seems as certain as the return of spring.

NEWCOMERS TO BULBS

As newcomers to bulb growing, we usually start with tulips or daffodils, the two best-known species, but soon discover there's a huge range of others to try. Before long, we've grown Crocuses, tried Nerines and Sparaxis and are starting to search for suppliers of even stranger and more exotic species that call to us from the pages of picture books and catalogues. We forget these species may not suit our climate. It does not matter that we'll have to go to extraordinary lengths to flower them; we have seen them and want them, even if for only one season.

Other types of plants have their enthusiasts but no other group captures the hearts of so many people as do bulbs.

WHAT IS A BULB?
(And does it matter?)

Botanically speaking, a bulb is one of four underground food storage structures some plants have. However, in this book we'll use the term to encompass all four structures – bulbs, corms, tubers and rhizomes. That's what gardeners do because, whether a plant has a bulb rather than a corm, tuber or rhizome, makes little difference to the way we grow and use them. If you'd like to know more about the structure of the four organs, read the information on page 6. Each structure is quite different, which can be helpful in the identification of unknown species or when botanists are deciding to which family a plant belongs.

They are all bulbs to us

From a gardener's point of view, the botanical differences between bulbs, corms, tubers and rhizomes make no difference. They are all planted and grown in the same way and can be freely mixed like this delightfully diverse combination, including cormous Anemones and bulbous tulips.

What's the difference?

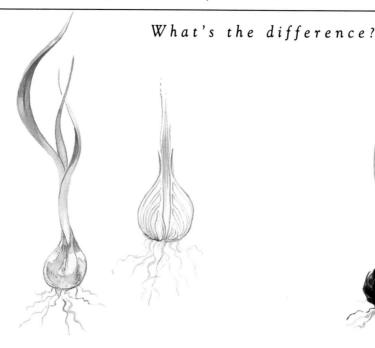

True bulbs

True bulbs are droplet shaped, although some are quite squat, and consist of a flower bud surrounded by fleshy, immature leaves, each wrapping around or overlapping the one below and all attached to a thickened base from which roots grow. Stems and flowers emerge from the pointy top. Most bulbs have a dry, peeling or flaking outer covering.

Corms

Corms are the swollen remains of last year's stems. They come in round or flat shapes and without the "onion rings" of bulbs. Stems emerge from the top of the corm, roots from the base. A new corm develops on top of the old, where the stem emerges, and tiny cormlets may form around the base.

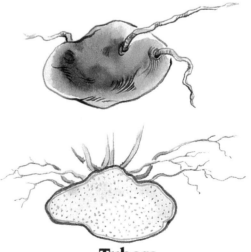

Rhizomes

Rhizomes are extensions of the stem which usually grow underground, as in ginger, but may creep along the surface, as in some Iris. They are branched, flattened cylinders with tips from which new growth emerges. Rhizomes that have flowered will not do so again, so when dividing them, replant only the young, new sections.

Tubers

Tubers are either enlarged sections of stems or swollen parts of roots, depending on the species. Cut in half, a tuber has a uniform consistency with no signs of internal organs – a potato is a familiar example. New growth springs either from "eyes" scattered over the surface, as in potatoes, or from buds at one end, as in Dahlias.

Climates for Bulbs

THEIR STRANGE AND SEASONAL NEEDS

In their natural places, plants must cope with the extremes of their native area's climate. Many parts of the world have at least one season which is hostile to, and dangerous for, unprotected life. Frigid winters can kill plants and animals, as can hot, very dry summers. But in the natural world, they adapt to their environment; animals grow then shed fur, migrate to more congenial climes, or hibernate.

Plants also protect themselves against extremes of climate. Some plants, such as annual flowers, avoid them entirely by completing their whole lives in the milder seasons. Others protect their leaves beneath thick, waxy cuticles; examples of these include some conifers and cacti or succulent plants. Then there are plants which choose to shed their leaves and become dormant. Most bulbs are in the latter category. When hard times approach, be it a freezing and/or dry winter or a hot, dry summer, their leaves wither and all their energies are withdrawn into the bulb, to be released again when conditions inevitably improve. The bulb – or corm, tuber or rhizome – is a food store that keeps the spark of life burning until conditions above the ground are safe.

As a group, bulbs are so tuned into the seasonal changes in their native lands that they *need* to experience those changes to flower and function properly. And that's where problems can start for gardeners.

Life cycle of a spring-flowering bulb

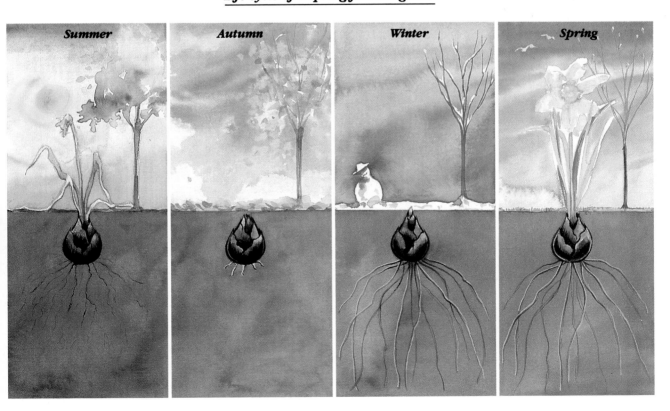

| Summer | Autumn | Winter | Spring |

REFRIGERATING BULBS

What does it do?

Spring-flowering bulbs come onto the market anytime from late summer. That is too early to plant them, even in cold areas. In warm areas, it may be four months too early.

So what do you do with them? Start by leaving them in the nursery until later in autumn; the bulb-selling season is not short.

After buying the bulbs you can place them in the crisper bin of the fridge* – not in the freezer – or store them in a cool, dark, airy place. Which one you choose depends on your climate. In cold areas where soil temperatures fall rapidly in autumn, put them straight in the fridge for six to eight weeks. After that, soil temperatures should be low enough to permit outdoor planting of the bulbs. Alternatively, buy the bulbs later in autumn and plant them straight into a cool soil.

In frost-free and warmer climates, your soil temperature** won't be cool enough to accept cold-climate bulbs until at least the first month of winter. In this case, store bulbs in a cool, totally dark, airy place until about mid-autumn. Then transfer them to the fridge for six to eight weeks. If you plan to grow them in pots, plant them in refrigerated potting mix, then refrigerate the potted bulbs for a further six to eight weeks, giving a total cooling of 12 to 16 weeks.

Never store bulbs in plastic; use paper or net bags, or arrange in a single layer on a tray.

Refrigerating dry bulbs simulates their natural growing conditions and initiates processes that lead to root and flower formation. Remember, cold-climate bulbs must be planted in cold soil – under 11°C (52°F) to develop roots – hence the need for refrigerated potting mix and to refrigerate the potted bulbs in warm climates.

No refrigeration or cool storage is necessary for warm-climate bulbs. They can be planted whenever they are available. In cold climates, winter-growing bulbs from warm climates must be grown in heated greenhouses.

*Label refrigerated bulbs clearly as some are poisonous and must not be mistaken for onions.

**More on the importance of soil temperature at planting time follows on page 17.

GET TO KNOW YOUR CLIMATE
And theirs

If the bulb you want to grow comes from a climate that is a lot different to yours, it may not do well without considerable help from you. You may have to artificially create the temperatures and seasonal changes in moisture that the bulb expects. That usually rules out growing them in the garden, so enthusiasts raise them in pots. These can be sheltered from rain when the bulb expects dryness, and even refrigerated to simulate a cold winter.

IN COLD CLIMATES
Tender bulbs freeze

Gardeners in areas where winters are always long and deeply frosty accept that a plant native to a frost-free climate won't survive long if grown unprotected. Bulbs from warm parts of the world cannot be left in the ground during winter in Britain, Canada and the colder parts of the USA. They must be lifted each autumn and stored indoors above freezing point until the soil warms up in spring. Left where they are, they'd simply freeze to death.

These are known as "tender" bulbs. In the wild they can accept the odd light to moderate frost, perhaps even a light snowfall for a day or two at a time. But they have no ability to withstand deep freezes or even near-freezing temperatures that go on for weeks or months. In their homelands, winter nights may be mostly frosty but days are usually sunny and warm, much warmer than winter days in the UK, Canada and northern USA.

Gardeners in cold climates have no trouble with warm-climate bulbs that begin their cycle in spring and are dormant in autumn but, without a heated greenhouse, those that grow through winter will be out of the question.

IN WARM CLIMATES
Upsets for the hardy

Unfortunately, many warm-climate gardeners don't readily accept that the reverse of this situation is also true. Bulbs from cold climates or "hardy" bulbs – including tulips, daffodils, Crocuses, Fritillarias and many more of the most desirable spring-flowering species – are not well suited to warm areas. These include places like the east and west coasts of Australia and South Africa, coastal northern New Zealand, coastal southern California and coastal regions of the Gulf and south-eastern States of the USA.

Such regions do not experience the long, frosty winters and low soil temperatures these bulbs expect, and need. With the exception of southern California and the west coasts of Australia and South Africa, these regions also receive a lot of their rain in summer, when the bulbs are expecting dryness. These exotic climates upset the natural rhythm of cold-climate bulbs, effectively turning them from long-lived perennials into annuals (plants that live for a single season).

MEDITERRANEAN CLIMATE
Rich in bulbs

Many of the world's bulbs come from areas that have a Mediterranean climate. This type of climate experiences wet winters and hot, dry, or near dry, summers. Winters can be either frost-free with minimums above freezing, cool with minimums down to -10˚C (14˚F), or cold with minimums below -10˚C (14˚F). Where winters are frost-free, they are rainy. Where they are cool, there may be some or several snowfalls, but where they are cold, most if not all of the winter rain falls as snow.

This latter type of Mediterranean climate is very severe. When snow begins to replace the late autumn rains, no more moisture soaks into the soil; moisture is held on top of the ground, frozen. The soil below is dry, being rewetted only when the snow melts in spring. When this occurs, bulbs start to shoot, using the food reserves in the bulb to grow much faster than would otherwise be possible. By comparison, annual and perennial flowers can only grow as fast as they can manufacture food through photosynthesis.

Quick growth is important for these Mediterranean climate bulbs because, although there will be some rain in early spring, the season is short, soon replaced by heat and dryness which withers the foliage and sends the bulb back into dormancy until the following spring.

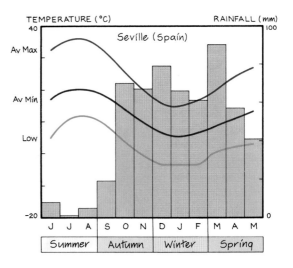

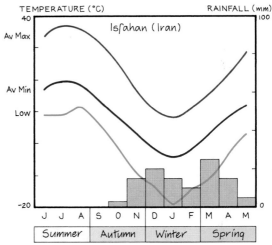

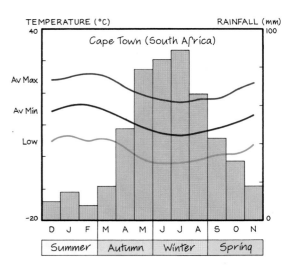

Mediterranean climates are home to more bulbs than any other climate. Within that climate there is much local variation, as these graphs show. Seville and Cape Town have at least some rain in summer; Isfahan has four rainless summer months, a low total annual rainfall and very low winter temperatures.

The climate where you live

The world's climate has been divided into broad zones of similarity. Knowing the characteristics of your climate helps you to choose bulbs and other plants that will have the greatest chance of success in your garden.

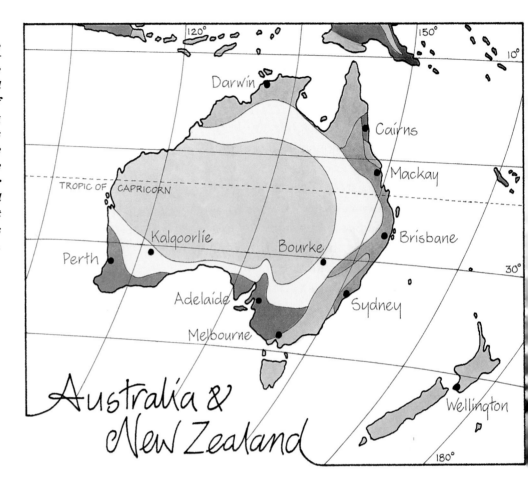

Australia & New Zealand

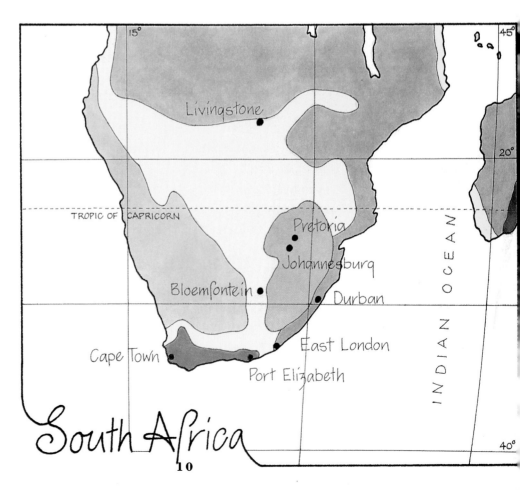

South Africa

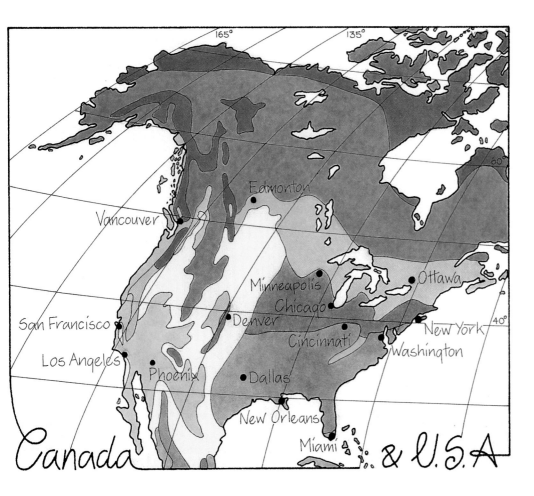

Canada & U.S.A

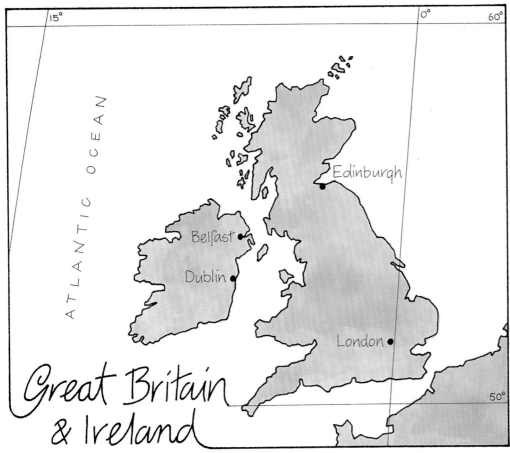

Great Britain & Ireland

ATLANTIC OCEAN

Key to map:

TUNDRA

Average summer temperature 0°-10°C (32°-50°F). Very severe winters.

SUB-ARCTIC

Severe winters. Average temperature above 10°C (50°F) for less than four months.

COLD CONTINENTAL

Rain year-round or dry winters. Average summer temperatures below 22°C (72°F).

COOL CONTINENTAL

Severe winters, warm to hot summers. May be dry in winter.

TEMPERATE

Cool winters, warm to hot summers. May be dry in winter.

SUBTROPICAL

Mild winters, warm to hot summers. May be rainy year-round or dry in winter.

MEDITERRANEAN

Cold to mild winters, warm to hot summers. Summers always dry.

SEMI-ARID

Relatively low rainfall . Cold, cool or mild winters.

DESERT

Very low rainfall. Winters may be cold or mild.

SEASONAL TROPICAL

Always above 18°C (64°F). High rainfall, heaviest in summer. Winters may be dry or less wet.

RAINY TROPICAL

Hot and humid year-round. Rain falls in every month.

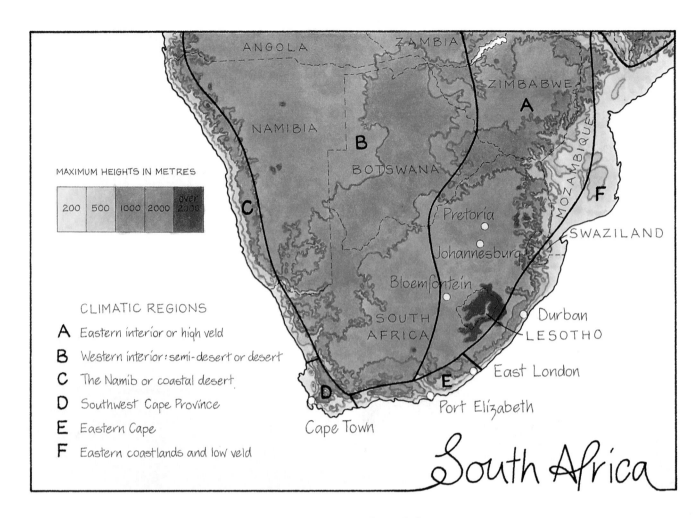

| 200 | 500 | 1000 | 2000 | over 2000 |

CLIMATIC REGIONS

A   Eastern interior or high veld

B   Western interior: semi-desert or desert

C   The Namib or coastal desert

D   Southwest Cape Province

E   Eastern Cape

F   Eastern coastlands and low veld

Elevation and rainfall

South Africa is a highland country with most land lying above 1000m (3300ft). Overnight lows of -10℃ (14℉) are possible in winter in inland and elevated parts. Areas C and D have a Mediterranean climate with most rain falling in autumn, winter and early spring. Area E and the western half of B receive rain at any time, although total rainfall in area B is very low. Areas A and F receive most of their rain in summer. The bulk of South Africa's bulbs come from areas C and D.

Bulbs from cold-winter, Mediterranean climates are the hardest to grow in places where winters are mild to warm and summers rainy. In such climates, they are most successful when planted in pots that are then refrigerated for eight to 12 weeks to simulate their natural winter conditions. Even then, they still won't flower more than once and should be discarded after blooming.

OTHER CLIMATES WITH BULBS

W e t   s u m m e r s ,   m i l d   w i n t e r s

Luckily, there are also bulbs that are native to other climatic regions, including those with cool to cold winters followed by humid, rainy summers; cool, dry winters followed by wet summers; and climates that are mild and rainy year-round. Southern Africa, for example, is home to more bulbs than any other region. For the warm-climate gardener, the southern tip of the Dark Continent has a wide choice of bulbs, but be aware that South Africa has zones with winter rainfall (a Mediterranean climate) and humid, sub-tropical regions that receive summer rain. The bulk of South Africa's bulbs are from the Cape region which has a Mediterranean climate.

It is important to choose species from the zone that's most like your climate. But don't be afraid to experiment. If your soil drains well, summer rain is usually harmless. You should also know that almost all of South Africa is highlands. Over 90 per cent of the country lies between 500 and 2000m (1600-6600ft) above sea level with most of this being over 1000m (3300 ft). This means that, despite its position in the subtropics, nights can be cool to cold in much of South Africa.

Other mild to warm parts of the world where bulb species are found include Australasia, South America, the southern USA and even a few parts of the tropics. Many of these bulbs are evergreen, happily accepting year-round rain, but not heavy or frequent frosts. Other bulbs can accept cool, moderately frosty winters, as long as the summers are warm and moist. Then there are the bulbs which remain dormant during the warmer months and grow during autumn and a mild winter.

Lowland tropical climates – and those with mild winters and rain in every month – are home to relatively few bulbs. These places – including the east coasts of Australia and South Africa and southern parts of the USA – are the hardest places in which to grow bulbs, especially those species from cold winter/dry-summer climates which need winter chilling.

THE BOTTOM LINE ON CLIMATE

But what does all this talk of climate mean? Simply this: if you want bulbs that will grow and flower every year with minimum effort, choose those from a climate that is similar to yours. The more extreme the difference, the more time and effort you will have to put in to ensure success. Bulb enthusiasts who are willing to artificially provide the temperature extremes and seasonal changes in moisture can virtually grow what they like – probably not in the garden but certainly in pots.

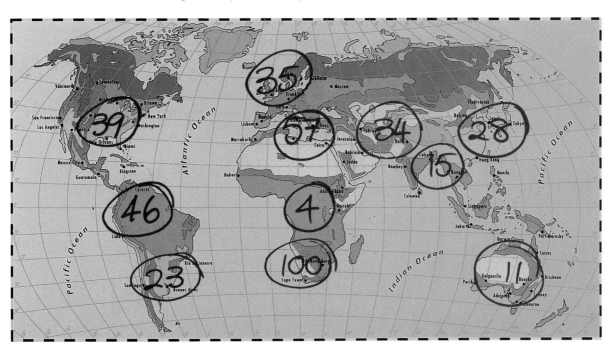

WHERE BULBS COME FROM

Origin of the species worldwide

There are bulbs native to every continent but the vast majority have evolved in places where at least one season is extreme. Most bulbs are found around the Mediterranean and in a band of similar climate that stretches into central Asia. South Africa has more species than any other single country. This map shows the number of species found in different regions.

Planting Bulbs

SOIL TEMPERATURE AND CONDITIONS

As a group, bulbs are not overly fussy about the type of soil they will grow in as long as the soil is very well drained. Most bulbs will quickly rot in soil that stays sodden and this is doubly true when they are dormant.

If you get a lot of your rain in the warmer half of the year but you want to grow bulbs from dry summer climates, you won't succeed without rapid soil drainage. For information on testing your soil's drainage, see the box at right.

SOILS FOR BULBS
It pays to improve it

Like other plants, bulbs will always grow best in good-quality, fertile soil, although they will tolerate a lot less than this. A pH of about 6.5 – that is, almost neutral, just a little on the acidic side – suits most bulbs. But there are exceptions, and we will note them in the individual descriptions of bulbs. For more details on soil pH, see the box at right.

If you are planning to plant a lot of bulbs in the one place, it will pay you to improve the soil by digging it over deeply, incorporating very well-rotted manure or compost as you go. It is important not to use fresh manure or to allow fertiliser granules to touch the bulbs as both can burn emerging roots. If in doubt, water the prepared bed thoroughly and let it lie for a month before planting bulbs. This gives the manure and fertiliser time to break down.

CLAY AND SAND
Problems and solutions for both

During digging, you may discover that your soil is largely heavy, sticky clay, in which case, digging in rotted organic matter and sand to make it friable and free-draining will be hard work. The amounts of additives needed to improve heavy clay will also be considerable, about 60 per cent of the volume of the soil in question.

An easier strategy is to enclose your garden beds with low retaining walls 20-25cm (8-10in) tall. Just break up the surface of the

---

DRAINAGE

Testing soil drainage

Dig a hole about 25cm (10in) deep, fill it with water and allow it to drain. Do this two or three times then refill again and time how long it takes to drain away. If water remains after 24 hours you have a drainage problem and the more water that remains, the worse it is.

You can improve soil drainage by installing a subsurface drainage system, by digging in a lot of sand, or by raising the level of garden beds behind retaining walls at least 20-25cm (8-10in) high.

ACIDIC AND ALKALINE SOILS

The pH scale

The pH is a measure of acidity and its opposite, alkalinity. It is measured on a scale of 1 to 14, with 1 being extreme acidity and 14 being extreme alkalinity. The midpoint, 7, is neutral, being neither acidic nor alkaline. Most plants enjoy a soil pH of between 5.5 and 7. Bulbs that grow on chalky or limey soils expect an alkaline soil of between 7 and 8.5. Acidic soil-lovers will tolerate a pH of 4.5 (strongly acidic). Digging in lime will raise the pH of soil (making it more alkaline). Adding sulphur will acidify it. It would be worth your while to buy a soil-testing kit or meter to determine the pH of your own garden soil.

Fussy beauty

*You'll need well-drained,
peaty soil to succeed with
these spectacular,
cold-climate Nomocharis.*

Cold comfort

*Cold-climate bulbs like
these vivacious 'Oxford'
tulips must be planted
in cool soil.*

existing clay soil, then raise the garden beds to the top of the walls by filling with good-quality, free-draining soil bought from a landscape supplier. Raised above the surrounding ground level, the new soil will be well drained and more fertile.

SANDY SOIL

If you have very sandy soil, you're in luck. Although sand is infertile, bulbs love its free-draining qualities. It is easy to dig, too, so working in a lot of well rotted manure or compost to improve its fertility is no problem. Note, though, that you will have to continuously mulch sandy soil with rotted organic matter as previous applications are used up or washed through the soil.

Most gardeners will have soil that is perfectly adequate, needing nothing more than regular applications of rotted organic matter – good garden practice whatever you are growing.

LAY MULCH EVERY YEAR
It's vital for soil health

It's a good idea to apply a layer of organic mulch to the surface of any type of soil after planting and at least once annually thereafter. Mulch conserves soil moisture, helps to form humus and improves the structure of soil. It also helps to stabilise the soil's temperature. In cold climates, a thick layer of mulch acts like a blanket, minimising repeated freezing and thawing of the soil which moves the buried bulbs and can break their roots. In hot climates, the mulch absorbs the sun's heat, keeping the soil below cooler, moister and more congenial to bulbs.

Mulch is composted (or rotted) organic matter. It could be grass clippings, shredded prunings, manure, straw, peanut shells, compost, wood shavings – in fact, any part or by-product of any living thing can be composted and turned into soil-improving mulch. But be careful not to use fresh, uncomposted matter as this can have an ill-effect on the soil while it is rotting down.

Apply up to 8cm (3in) mulch over tall-growing bulbs and no more than 3cm (1in) over low-growing bulbs. To protect all bulbs in the ground

from extreme heat or cold, cover with 15cm (6in) or more mulch as soon as the bulbs are dormant. Scrape away to the above depths before they re-emerge.

WHEN TO PLANT BULBS
Timing varies

Generally, bulbs should be planted when they are dormant – usually in autumn for spring-flowering bulbs or early spring for summer flowers. Evergreen species should be planted when they are least actively growing. But there are a few important exceptions to these generalisations and they will be noted in individual entries.

SOIL TEMPERATURE

Traditional, spring-flowering bulbs – daffodils, tulips, Crocuses, hyacinths and all other cold-climate, early-spring-flowering bulbs – can be damaged by being planted in soil that is too warm for them. Therefore, do not rush into planting them as soon as autumn arrives; wait until the temperature of the soil, at the depth of planting needed, has fallen to 11°C (52°F).

In the cooler parts of the globe – such as southern Canada, northern USA, the UK or mountainous parts of other countries – this may occur during the latter parts of the first month of autumn. In frost-free or near frost-free places, you may have to wait until the first month of winter.

Gardeners in mild to warm areas should buy a thermometer to determine the temperature of their soil. Dig a hole to the planting depth that the desired bulbs require, place the thermometer in it and backfill, being careful not to put the warmer topsoil in the bottom of the hole. Do this after dark and retrieve the thermometer after an hour or so.

In parts of Australia, South Africa, southern California and the southern and far south-eastern States of the USA, soil temperatures may never drop to anything like 11°C (52°F). If this is the case where you live, you should forget cold-climate spring bulbs (except in refrigerated pots) and instead choose from the many beautiful warm-climate varieties.

Even if you refrigerate the bulbs before planting, placing them into soil or potting mix that is too warm will prevent the bulbs from making good roots. And it usually destroys the flower buds within the bulbs.

Cold-climate bulbs need 8-14 weeks of these low soil temperatures to produce adequate roots and flower well. If your soil cools to 11°C (52°F) or less but only for a week or two, you will still fail with these bulbs.

Bulbs from frost-free or near frost-free climates require no such chilling; out-of-season wetness is their main enemy.

HOW TO PLANT THEM
Err on the side of deepness

The depth at which you plant bulbs in the garden is important but not critical. You will usually get full planting instructions from a commercial supplier. However, generally in friable loam, plant the bulb so that its top is two to three times the length of the bulb from the surface. If your soil is heavier, with more clay, plant a little more shallowly. In light, sandy soil you can plant more deeply. Usually, planting too deeply is better than planting too shallowly.

SUN, SHADE AND BULBS
How much light do they need?

Generally, bulbs require high light levels and most are happiest in full sun. But as always in gardening, there are a number of ifs and buts. If you live in a hot, sunny climate, the light will be more intense than in a cool-climate area.

The hotter and more sunny your climate, the brighter the light and the more shade your bulbs can tolerate, especially those that are native to high latitudes in the northern hemisphere. But, as bulbs always do best in a climate that is similar to the one from which they come, sensible warm-climate gardeners will be growing those species from climates similar to theirs – and growing them in full sun.

If you must plant bulbs in the shade, choose a spot with the least amount of shade at the time of year when the bulbs have leaves. Levels of shade are irrelevant when the bulbs are dormant.

Left: Generally, bulbs in gardens should be planted at a depth twice their length, to the tip of the bulb, beneath the soil.

Above: Some bulbs, however, prefer to have their noses poking above the soil.

Above, right: Others need from 1/3 to 1/2 their length above soil level.

POINTS ABOUT PLANTING

Finding cool spots in hot gardens

♦ Plant in shade

Gardeners in warm climates who are determined but struggling to grow cold-climate bulbs can maximise their chances of success by planting them in the coolest soil they have. This could be found on the shady side of the house (the southern side in the southern hemisphere, the northern side in the north). Bulbs prefer full sun but the shade cast by a building is not as dense as that from an overhanging tree, and in hot, sunny climates, even indirect light is bright enough for bulbs used to the softer light of higher latitudes.

♦ Plant deeply

Another way to keep bulbs cooler in warm areas is to plant them 20cm (8in) deep. The soil there is cooler than that nearer the surface. This only seems to work if you live in an area that's just outside the range of cold-climate bulbs, not well outside it. Only plant the larger bulbs at this depth; small bulbs may not have the strength to reach the surface.

♦ Mulch helps, but...

A thick layer of mulch will also help to keep the soil below cool; however, remember that mulch is not a miracle substance. In a very warm climate, it won't keep a site which slopes towards the sun cool enough for cold-climate bulbs.

♦ Plant on a slope

If your land or part of it slopes away from the sun (towards the south or south-east in the southern hemisphere, towards the north or north-east in the north), the soil on this slope will be a lot cooler than if it sloped towards the sun or was flat. The more steeply it slopes away, the cooler it will be.

♦ Give up!

If you've tried everything but still can't get a good result from daffodils or tulips, give up and try warm-climate bulbs instead. The only thing you're doing wrong is trying to force your climate onto bulbs that don't like it.

On the other hand...

Warm spots in cool gardens

If you live in a climate that is a little too cold for winter-growing bulbs, you may still have a microclimate that would suit them. Conditions at the foot of a masonry wall, a fence or a rockery that receives full sun all day in winter will be considerably warmer than those in more exposed parts of the garden. Such sites may be suitable for bulbs that would otherwise be considered tender, especially if the soil is also mulched. You could also try planting tender bulbs deeply, so as to insulate them from freezing temperatures, or plant them in soil that slopes towards the sun.

LIFTING BULBS

How to ensure consistent flowering

When clumps of bulbs in your garden become so overcrowded that the number and quality of flowers is reduced, it's time to lift, separate and replant.

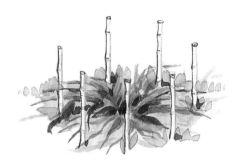

Step 1
Before leaves die back completely, define the outer edges of the clump with several small stakes.

Step 2
When the leaves are gone, dig around the clump with a spade to separate it from the soil.

Step 3
Now use a fork to lift the clump out of the ground. Shake off as much excess soil as you can.

Step 4
A congested clump may consist of hundreds of bulbs. Take it to a shady place where you can comfortably separate and clean the bulbs.

Step 5
Refurbish the planting site by digging in old manure or compost and some complete plant food.

Lifting Bulbs

A PROCEDURE TO KEEP FLOWERS COMING

If you choose bulbs that suit your climate, almost all of them can be planted and left with little attention except for an occasional feeding and removal of spent flowers.

However, some of the most popular bulbs – hybrid tulips (the typical ones) and hyacinths among them – should be dug up each year after blooming, even when they are growing in an ideal climate. Individual entries in the following chapters will indicate whether or not this is necessary.

If you choose bulbs that do not suit your climate, they need to be lifted and stored every year after blooming to escape that part of your climate to which they are unsuited. If you are unsure whether a particular species suits your climate, leave them in the garden and see whether there are more flowers the following year. If there are not, the plants are going backwards.

LIFT & SEPARATE
Preventing congestion

Eventually, all bulbs grown in pots and garden beds, rather than those naturalised in large spaces, will need to be lifted, separated and replanted in refurbished soil. This is because, as the bulbs increase in number beneath the soil, the clump becomes congested. As the individual bulbs compete for water, food and root space, some lose out, so flowers decline in number, size and quality. Typically, you will need to lift and separate every three to five years, depending on the vigour of the bulbs and the amount of space left between them when planted.

Successful naturalised bulbs also become congested but as there are so many of them in that sort of broad-scale planting, the number, size and quality of flowers is not important enough to warrant the huge task of lifting and dividing.

WHEN & HOW TO LIFT
It's a relatively easy task

Lift bulbs when they are dormant or, in the case of evergreens, when they are least actively growing.

When you decide that lifting is necessary, mark the outer edges of the clump before the leaves die completely. Then you will know where to dig without slicing or piercing bulbs.

Use a sharp spade to free the clump from the surrounding soil, then lift with a garden fork. Shake off the excess soil and take the clump to a place where you can comfortably separate, sort and inspect the bulbs. Retain the biggest and healthiest for replanting; discard any that show signs of rot or damage.

If the bulbs like being where they have been growing, there will be many, possibly hundreds of small bulbs attached to the clump. You can use these to grow more clumps of that bulb, pot some up, or give them away. Otherwise, simply discard the excess. Don't feel guilty about this; vigorously growing bulbs will always reproduce at a far greater rate than the average gardener can use. It's a sign that you're doing everything right. Dispose of the excess bulbs properly; never plant or dump them in natural bushland as they may become a damaging environmental weed.

Before replanting the retained bulbs, dig up the area, adding plenty of rotted organic matter as you dig. It is not essential to replant dormant bulbs immediately; they can be stored in a cool, dark, airy place until their usual planting time.

Growing Bulbs

IN TURF, UNDER TREES OR IN POTS

Bulbs which grow and flower in early spring, then die back to ground, are sometimes seen growing in clumps in lawns. Daffodils and related Narcissus (jonquils) are the most popular choices for this treatment.

The effect is charming but, as the leaves of the bulbs must be left intact for about eight weeks after blooming, the grass amongst the clump cannot be cut until at least late spring. Where winters are cool to cold this isn't a problem; cool-climate grasses only begin to grow in mid to late spring, so they won't be excessively long and untidy before the yellowed leaves can be mown away.

In warmer climates this is not the case. The grass here can grow even in winter and, well before it's time to cut the bulb leaves, the grass will be overlong. The grass looks unsightly and smothers the bulb leaves, reducing their ability to feed the bulb below. You can mow the grass beyond the clump at any time but, in a warm climate, you may have to hand-snip the grass surrounding the bulbs until the bulb's leaves have turned yellow. Don't snip the bulb leaves; while they're green they're producing next year's flowers.

BULBS IN TURF
How to plant them

The easiest way to establish a clump of bulbs beneath grass is to cut a rectangle of turf with a sharp spade and roll it back like a rug. Dig out the exposed soil to a depth much greater than the planting depth of the bulbs. Backfill to the right depth with a mixture of the excavated soil and rotted organic matter. Place the bulbs in a random group and cover with more of the soil/organic matter mix until the original soil level is reached. Tamp down and water well, adding more soil if there is slumping. Re-lay the grass and water again.

The bulbs won't appear for many weeks but it is vital that you know where they are and examine the site frequently for signs of their appearance. Mow the grass for the last time as soon as you see the first sign of a shoot and keep a note of the date this occurred for next year.

When lots of shoots are visible, feed the clump with complete plant food or bulb food.

Cut off flowers as they fade so as not to waste the bulb's energies on unwanted seed production, but leave the flower stem intact to help feed the bulb. As the leaves are also feeding the bulb, do not cut these until they have turned yellow. If you do, you will have few, if any, flowers next year. Don't forget the soil must be cool before you plant cold-climate bulbs.

BULBS UNDER TREES
Which species to choose

As a rule, bulbs will not grow and flower successfully under the full shade of a tree, although it is possible to grow some species beneath deciduous trees. The bulbs to choose are species that appear in late winter or early spring while deciduous trees are still dormant and leafless. Good choices include bluebells, daffodils and Crocuses, although any bulb with a winter and spring growth habit is worth a try. Bulbs with a summer growth habit, such as lilies, will not grow and flower well under deciduous trees because the shade cast in summer is too dense.

In warmer climates, some cool-climate bulbs – bluebells, for instance – can grow successfully

Select your spot and prepare

Step 1.
Cut a rectangle in the grass with a sharp spade.

Step 2.
Slide spade under grass and roll turf back.

Step 3.
Dig out the soil to a depth of about 30cm (12in).

Step 4.
**Backfill to the planting depth with a
mixture of the dug soil and compost or
old manure and fertiliser. Place bulbs in a
random pattern and cover with improved
soil to restore original level. Water to settle,
adding more soil if slumping occurs. Roll
back the grass, and water again.**

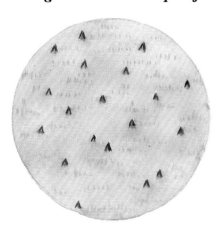

**Step 5.
Mow the
grass for the
last time when
the very first
sign of a
shoot
appears.**

under open, lightly foliaged evergreen trees where they appreciate the dappled shade and cooler soil. But remember, evergreen trees, being active year-round, will compete strongly for soil nutrients and water.

RANDOM PATTERNS

For a convincing naturalised drift under trees you will need at least 50 bulbs. A mass of the one type always looks good, but you could experiment with a mixture of two or three types as long as they all grow and flower before the trees produce too much shade.

To create a natural-looking, random pattern, gently toss the bulbs into the target area and plant them where they fall, even if several land next to each other.

Dig generously sized planting holes so that the developing roots can easily penetrate the soil. Work in some complete plant food or bulb fertiliser; cover this mixture with unfertilised soil to shield the bulb from direct contact with the fertiliser.

The bulbs will develop root systems during autumn and winter, long before you see top growth, so be sure to water the area if rain is unreliable.

Bulbs in Pots

A wonderful way to raise them

Almost all bulbs can be grown in pots and this is often the ideal way to raise them. They can be moved to the best site in the garden when in bloom, or can even be brought into the house. After blooming, they can be stored out of sight in a garage or shed. Away from the garden, they won't receive water when they don't want it and there's no chance of accidentally damaging the dormant bulbs while digging. Pots are usually the only option for gardeners wishing to grow bulbs from climates very dissimilar to their own because, in pots, they can be sheltered from out-of-season rain and even refrigerated if necessary.

Good drainage is vital to bulbs, so ensure that the pots chosen have large drainage holes. Plastic, metal or glazed ceramic pots are waterproof and dry out relatively slowly. Terracotta pots are porous and lose water through their sides and drainage holes. If you use terracotta, you will have to water more often – and feed more often – as watering washes nutrients out of the potting mix. Terracotta pots that dry out in summer can be fatal to summer growers.

Planting bulbs in pots

1. Fill the container with enough potting mix so that, when bulbs are placed on top, their tips will be about 1cm (½ in) below the rim.

2. Place bulbs close together but don't let them touch each other or the pot. The pot must be full for the best display.

3. Shake potting mix over the bulbs and firm down between them. Sprinkle with water to settle the soil, adding more mix if necessary. The tips should appear just above the surface.

Pretty in pots

*Yellow lily-flowered tulips
and blue forget-me-nots
make a brilliant splash of
spring colour in a big pot.
Almost all bulbs can do
this for you, either in the
garden or indoors in bloom.*

HEATSTROKE DANGER

Heat is another factor to consider with pots. If you place a pot of bulbs in full sun, the sunny side of the pot will absorb heat. This dries the potting mix quickly and can overheat the bulbs so much that they fail to flower. This is especially likely to happen with potted cold-climate bulbs, such as tulips. To prevent this, place the pot within another, bigger pot or cane basket.

SHAPE OF POTS

Whatever the material of the pot, a wide, shallow dish offers the best display opportunities, but you should know that a fixed amount of soil in the bottom of all pots stays waterlogged for some time after watering. It doesn't matter whether the pot is deep or shallow, about the same depth of soil remains sodden for a long time. Therefore, the taller the pot, the more free-draining soil there is for the bulbs' roots.

If you like to use wide, shallow containers, you should pay particular attention to watering. Water

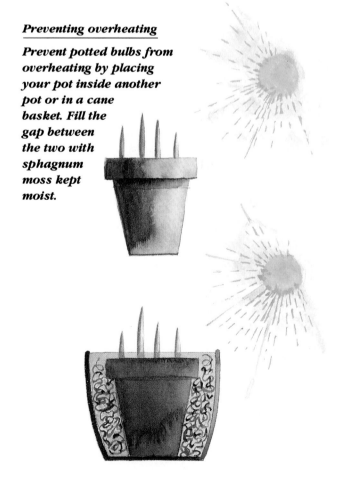

Preventing overheating

Prevent potted bulbs from overheating by placing your pot inside another pot or in a cane basket. Fill the gap between the two with sphagnum moss kept moist.

only when necessary, that is, when the top few centimetres of soil feels dry to the touch. During continuous rain, shelter the dish.

FORCING BULBS TO BLOOM

There is a difference between growing bulbs "naturally" in pots – that is, allowing them to grow and flower according to their usual timetable – and "forcing" bulbs to bloom at unnatural times. Traditional cool and cold-climate spring-flowering bulbs, such as daffodils, tulips, hyacinths, Crocuses, are often forced so that they bloom for indoor display in winter rather than spring.

In some countries, you can buy bulbs that have been prepared for forcing by the grower. Use prepared bulbs if you can get them as they will flower even earlier than unprepared ones. The bulbs are planted shallowly in the pots, usually with their tips just above the surface. They are also placed very close together, but not touching each other.

For good flowering in pots, forced bulbs must first make roots. Cool and cold-climate spring bulbs only make roots when the temperature of the potting mix is below 11°C (52°F), but above freezing. Root growth takes about nine weeks. If you don't live in a climate where there is a nine-week period when temperatures rarely rise above 11°C (52°F) even in the day, the potted bulbs need to be cooled in the fridge.

Flowering is sure to be disappointing if temperatures are so warm that potted, cool-climate bulbs start shooting well before adequate roots have formed. And, as these bulbs are potted with their pointed tips above soil level, it is important that the cooling period occurs in the dark, as if the bulbs were underground. Light and/or warmth will cause the bulbs to shoot prematurely.

If you live in a cold climate, leave the potted bulbs outside in the shade but cover the container to exclude light. Alternatively, dig a trench in cold soil, deeper than the depth of the pots, and place the pots in the trench. Cover with soil, ashes or mulch to exclude light. In warm climates, chilling the potted bulbs in the fridge keeps them cool and shaded. During the cooling and root-forming period, keep the potting mix lightly, evenly moist – not sodden and not dry.

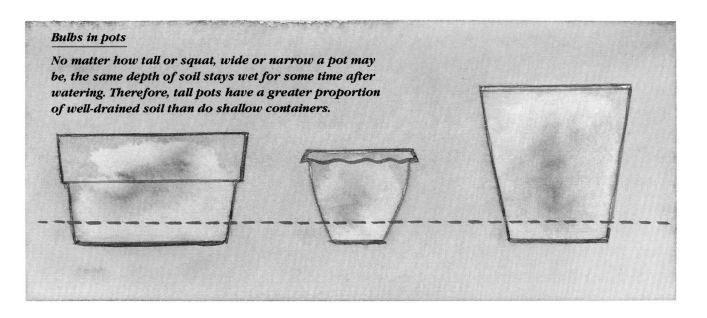

BRINGING THE POTS INDOORS

When bringing the pots out of the cold and dark, two other potential problems arise. The sudden rise in temperature that the bulbs will experience in a heated house or outside in a warm climate can cause gases that are toxic to the bulb to build up inside it. Therefore chilled bulbs should be acclimatised by being brought to their flowering site in two stages, the interim stage being warmer than the place of chilling but cooler than the final site. This interim spot should be light but not sunny, as full sun, even in late autumn or winter, can burn the new shoots.

For traditional spring bulbs in pots, the final flowering site should not be warmer than 14°C (57°F) at night and 18°C (64°F) in the day. Gardeners in warm areas may now understand why it can be so hard for them to successfully flower cool-climate bulbs, such as daffodils, tulips and Crocuses, even in pots and even when refrigerated.

In warm climates, only bring the bulbs indoors when flowers are about to open (about three to four weeks after removal from the chilling site). Never place these bulbs on top of TVs or near heaters. If possible, place in an unheated room overnight.

Forced spring bulbs will not reflower the following year and are best discarded. In cold climates, although they won't reflower in pots, they can be planted in the garden in spring to recover. It is usually at least two seasons before they return to normal flowering cycles. Don't bother with this in a warm climate as they won't grow for you anyway.

NATURAL FLOWERING IN POTS

Only bulbs that come from cold climates expect and need a chilling period. Those from warmer areas, such as South Africa, do not. They can be grown in pots without special treatment, other than a slightly more shallow planting depth than in the garden.

Given adequate food and water, they do not have to be discarded after blooming. However, planted very closely together (as you would for a good display), the multiplying bulbs usually fill the pot quickly, making unpotting, separating and replanting necessary every year or two.

You can unpot and separate the bulbs anytime after they have become dormant. Store the separated, cleaned bulbs in an airy, cool, dry, dark place until replanting time.

GROWING BULBS INDOORS

Bulbs are not indoor plants and, unless you have a room with a lot of glass that gets full sun for hours every day, do not attempt to grow the bulbs in the house. Grow them outside, bringing them in only when the flowers are opening.

A windowsill that faces the sun all day may do, but you will have to turn the pot every day to ensure even growth and exposure to the sun, and to prevent the flowers from appearing on an angle. Take care, also, to ensure that the pot itself does not overheat. See the section titled "Heatstroke Danger" on page 26 for details.

Propagating Bulbs

INCREASE YOUR STOCK SIMPLY AND INEXPENSIVELY

All bulbs create new bulbs as part of their reproduction cycle, although some produce more bulbs than others. After a few years in the ground, clumps of bulbs usually need to be dug up and replanted into refurbished soil. When you lift the clump, you will find anything from a few to hundreds more bulbs than you planted. For most gardeners, this increase will supply all the stock they could ever want.

SEPARATION
The easiest method of all

If the parent plant is a bulb or corm, bulblets or cormels simply separate from it. If good-sized, these will probably bloom in the next flowering season but smaller ones will need at least two seasons.

If the plant has a rhizome or tuber, you will have to cut it into sections. With rhizomes, retain only the young rhizomes with buds or leaves. Discard any that have flowered as they won't flower again. Cut rhizomes into 8-15cm (3-6in) sections so that each has buds or leaves and some roots. Replant these immediately, shallowly, into fertile, well-drained soil.

With tubers, the "eyes" or buds are the important parts. Dahlias, for example, form a cluster of tubers around the base of the stem of the plant. Separate each tuber with a sliver of old stem attached. Mid-spring is a good time to do this, when the eyes on the tubers are swelling, but before shoot growth occurs. After slicing the tubers apart, allow the wound to dry for a few days in a clean, dark, airy place before replanting.

Separating corms

Little cormels cluster around the base plate of parent corms. They can be separated but, because of their small size, may take two years to flower.

Separating rhizomes

Cut rhizomes into sections at least 8cm (3in) long. Use the young, new growths which have shoots or buds and some roots.

Separating tubers

Tubers cluster around the old stem or along the roots. Each can be separated to form a new plant. Each separated tuber should have a small sliver of old stem attached and some buds or eyes from which new growth will develop.

Separating bulbs

Young bulbs which are mature enough to separate will pull away easily from the parent.

Breeding brilliance

Bulbs that like your climate and conditions will multiply fast. If you succeeded with these pink Freesias, for instance, you could have a massed display within a few years.

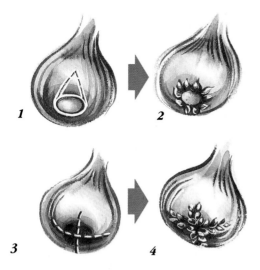

Scoring bulbs

1. Using a small, sharp knife, scoop out the entire base plate leaving a conical hole in the bulb.
2. In time, bulblets will form around the edge of the hole. They will take two or three years to bloom.
3. Alternatively, make two or three deep cuts across the base of the bulb.
4. In time, bulblets will form along the cuts. They will also take up to three years to bloom.

The seedling tray

Sow seed thinly onto a seedling tray full of commercial seed-raising mix. If seed is very fine, mix with a handful of dry sand and sprinkle the mixture over the tray. The sand helps to spread the seed and you can see where you've sown. Moisten and cover with a sheet of glass until germination.

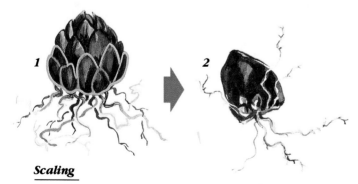

Scaling

1. Some bulbs have overlapping scales and these can be used to grow many new plants.
2. Remove the bottom two scale layers only from the parent plant and place in a plastic bag of moistened sphagnum, peat or vermiculite. Over time, bulblets will form on each scale.

SCALING

Beware of fungal diseases

Use the scaling method on bulbs consisting of overlapping scales, such as Lilium. Separate anytime from late summer through to the end of autumn.

Clean the lifted bulbs and separate the lowest row of scales from the base plate. If you need more bulbs, you can remove the second row from the base. This won't harm the parent bulb, but detaching many more rows will. If the parent bulb is expendable and you want a large number of new plants, take more scales.

As the separated scales are susceptible to fungal diseases, dust them with a fungicide powder. Have some moistened sphagnum, peatmoss or vermiculite handy – the material is just moist enough when you can't squeeze any more water from it. Put the moist medium and the scales in a plastic bag and seal it. Place the bag in a dark place for two months, then put it in the fridge for another ten weeks. After this time, the bulblets that have formed at the base of the scales can be potted.

SCORING

For use on onion-like bulbs

This technique, undertaken in early summer, successfully multiplies those bulbs that consist of onion-like, concentric rings, such as hyacinths, daffodils, jonquils, Allium, Nerine and Scilla.

Using a very sharp, sterile knife, slice out the entire base plate, leaving a deep, conical hole. Alternatively, make three or four deep, evenly spaced cuts across the base of the bulb. After a few days, the cuts will widen and you should dust the openings with fungicide powder to prevent infection.

Place the cut or scooped-out bulbs into half a plastic bag full of lightly moist vermiculite, sphagnum or peatmoss. Seal and place in a warm, dark spot until autumn, then remove the bulbs from the bag and plant in the garden. The bulblets will sprout in spring but the parent bulbs will die. Lift when the foliage withers, separate the bulblets and grow on. Don't expect flowers for at least two more years, possibly three.

Buying Bulbs

Where to buy them & what to look for

You can buy bulbs from garden centres or by mail order from specialist growers. Garden centres generally stock a small range of the most popular varieties. In early autumn, you will find daffodils, tulips and hyacinths at every nursery; some will have a wide choice. However, no garden centre carries the range of species or the choice of hybrids within a species that is offered by the bigger mail-order bulb specialists. These companies will send out to you a colour catalogue or a list of their offerings and you will usually get full growing instructions with your order.

The best way to locate mail-order bulb suppliers is to look through the advertisements in a gardening magazine. In autumn and spring, big companies will take full-page advertisements, but don't forget to scan the classifieds as well. Smaller operators, often growers specialising in rare or unusual bulbs, advertise there.

WHAT SIZE TO BUY

Often at garden centres in autumn you will see bins of loose bulbs. Sometimes they will be graded according to size – the bigger the bulb, the more or bigger the flower or flowers will be. If you want to grow the bulbs in pots or in a small planting in the garden, choose the biggest bulbs. They should feel quite heavy and not look shrivelled or damaged. If you want to buy a large number of bulbs for a massed display or to naturalise under trees, you will find the less expensive, smaller-sized bulbs adequate.

STORING YOUR BULBS

You can store bought bulbs in a cool, dark airy place until the time comes to plant them. Cold-climate, early-spring-flowering bulbs, such as daffodils and tulips, can be stored in paper or net bags in the crisper bin of the refrigerator. Chilling improves a bulb's performance, but remember, bulbs that need pre-chilling also need to be planted in cool soil – between 1-11°C (34-52°F) – anytime between the end of the first month of autumn and the start of winter, depending on where you live. If you plant in warmer soil, roots will not develop properly and flowering may be disappointing.

Don't refrigerate warm-climate bulbs; store them in a cool, dark, airy place.

SEEDLINGS

When you cannot obtain bulbs

All bulbs produce, and can be increased, by seed, but it can be a long wait between seedling and flower. As a rule, the bigger the bulb becomes, the longer the wait. Raising bulbs from seed, therefore, is really only viable when you cannot obtain the bulbs themselves. In mild to warm-climate areas some smaller bulbs – such as Freesias and Lapeirousias – will produce a few flowers in the first year from seed.

Start bulbs from seed either by sowing in seedling trays of fine, sandy seed-raising mix or directly into the garden. If you choose the latter course, a small vacant bed in a vegetable patch makes a better seedling nursery than an established garden bed; the little seedlings are less likely to be smothered by other plants.

Just bury seeds that can be picked up separately; dust-like seeds are best left on the surface of the seed-raising mix, misted with water and the whole tray covered with a sheet of glass or plastic film.

The seeds of bulbs which grow through the winter and flower in spring should be sown in autumn in cold areas or refrigerated for two months before sowing. When the seedlings have grown big enough to handle, either pot them in individual containers for growing on or space them out in a nursery bed in the garden. Transfer to their final site when they have grown to flowering size.

Pests and Diseases

HOW TO IDENTIFY AND CONTROL THEM

While bulbs are no more attractive to pests and diseases than any other big group of plants, there are so many of them, from such diverse regions of the world, that they have accumulated their fair share of natural enemies. Only a few of these pests and diseases, however, attack bulbs or types of bulbs exclusively. Most can be found on a wide range of other plants and you may already know them well. Restrain them on bulbs as you would on other plants. The use of pesticides and fungicides is controlled by government authorities, and what is allowed to be sold to home gardeners varies from one place to another. In this chapter, we will not suggest specific chemical remedies. Instead, use this guide to help you identify pests and diseases then seek the advice of your local nursery for an appropriate remedy. Before purchase, read the label to satisfy yourself that the chemical will control the problem in question and that it is safe to use on the affected plants.

PESTS

Vigilance is the best and most eco-friendly insurance against damage caused by pests. Gardeners who regularly inspect their plants will see the early signs of damage and can often end the problem at once, by hand. If a pesticide is necessary, use it strictly as directed.

Mites

Mites are very small and hard to see, except with a magnifying glass. There are several types, including two-spotted (red-spider) mites, Cyclamen mites and bulb mites. They mostly inhabit the undersides of leaves where they suck sap, causing a yellow mottling or silvering of the foliage and a decline in the vigour of the plant. Apart from these symptoms, the presence of mites is indicated by a very fine webbing beneath the leaves and in leaf joints.

Bulb mites attack the bulb itself, causing weak growth and deformed flowers. The bulbs may rot if severely infested.

In the garden, mites appear during the warmer months and can be a problem on summer-growing bulbs. They can live year-round in heated greenhouses. Unchecked, their numbers will increase rapidly, causing severe damage.

The best control of mites is achieved with several sprays 10-14 days apart, beginning mid-spring. Once numbers have built up, control is harder. Use a miticide and, as these pests can become resistant to chemicals, alternate between two different chemicals (not brands – the active ingredient is named on the label).

Alternatively, buy predatory mites and release onto affected plants. After release, do not spray with poisons.

If bulb mites are suspected, dip dug bulbs into miticide. Burn badly affected bulbs and do not replant in the same spot.

Eelworms/ Nematodes

These tiny, ground-dwelling pests attack bulbs directly, causing them to blacken. Affected bulbs feel soft and, if sliced in half, the rings inside will be dark. Leaves may also blister or develop uneven ridges or splits and appear bleached and deformed.

In frost-free climates, an eelworm attack can occur at any time of the year, but in colder areas they are most active during the warmer months. Burn all infected bulbs and don't replant bulbs in infested soil for at least three years.

Whitefly

These are very small, white flying insects which congregate in numbers, usually under the leaves. When disturbed they fly off as one, but quickly resettle.

Whiteflies suck sap and, in large numbers, cause the leaves to yellow and dry. They are easily controlled with an aerosol, all-purpose garden insecticide. Alternatively, paint a piece of bright yellow cardboard with light oil or petroleum jelly and hang or stand near affected plants. Whiteflies are attracted to yellow and will stick to the surface.

Mealy bugs

Slow-moving mealy bugs look like little blobs of cotton wool. They infest the roots and leaves of plants, hiding in leaf joints and on the undersides of foliage. Mealy bugs suck the sap, deforming flowers. Heavy infestations can weaken plants.

If pests are seen above ground, it's likely that roots will be infested, too. Systemic insecticide will control both. Alternatively, drench plants with contact insecticide applied with a watering can; apply enough insecticide to saturate the soil. Immerse potted plants or dug bulbs in an insecticide solution.

Aphids/Greenfly

These common pests may be green, black, pink or pale yellow. They can be seen in dense clusters on flower buds and soft new growth. They suck sap, withering or deforming flower buds and leaves. Serious viral diseases may also be transmitted from one plant to another by these insects.

Most prevalent during the warmer months, aphids appear along with fresh new growth and flower buds. They are often transported to new sites by ants which harvest the sweet honeydew excreted by aphids.

Ladybirds, lacewings and their young, hoverflies, parasitic wasps and some birds are natural enemies and the insects are easy to squash by hand. If spraying is necessary, use a low-toxicity pyrethrum or fatty-acid-based spray. Sprays will also kill the natural predators named above.

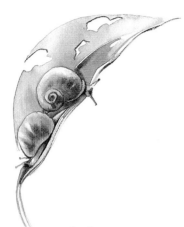

entire sections of the plant are consumed. Many caterpillars are active only at night, hiding during the day, while others are well camouflaged so the cause of the damage may not be apparent.

Look under leaves near the damage for them, and on leaves below damage for clues. Clusters of little black, green or brownish balls are caterpillar droppings.

If pests cannot be found and squashed, spray with *Bacillus thuringiensis*, a disease which affects only caterpillars.

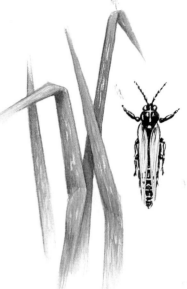

Snails and slugs

Worldwide pests familiar to every gardener, snails and slugs chew new foliage, strip the surface of stems and eat holes in the flowers and buds.

They are most active at night and on dewy mornings in late spring and early autumn. Apart from obvious damage, their presence is indicated by silvery trails left on plants and the ground surface.

Pick off and squash or drop into a bucket of very salty water. Alternatively, lay snail bait pellets or spray affected foliage with soluble formulation.

Bulb flies

This is a very destructive pest group, comprising two different species. Both cause similar damage and are controlled in the same way. Adult flies lay their eggs near the bulb or among its foliage as it is dying back. Maggots emerge and bore into the bulb, eating out the centre. Infested bulbs become soft and spongy, but this is not apparent until they are lifted.

Suspected infestations can be confirmed by cutting bulbs open – they will be full of maggots. Affected bulbs should be burned and unaffected nearby bulbs should be soaked in an insecticide solution.

Thrips

Very small, black and elongated, thrips can be seen moving about on flowers and the undersides of leaves. They break the surfaces of leaves and buds with their rasp-like mouths to get at the sap. This causes silvering, streaking, stunting and deformation.

Thrips are a serious pest of Gladiolus, Allium and many other bulbs. They are most prevalent in summer, especially if the weather is hot and dry.

Use a contact or systemic insecticide and spray at first sign of infestation, repeating at 10-day intervals. Rainy weather and high humidity can discourage them.

Stem borers

These pests bore into the stems of taller, summer bulbs, such as Dahlias, Liliums, Gladiolus and gingers, and eat out the interiors. Whole stems often collapse or leaves suddenly wither. Systemic insecticides may be effective if applied before or just after the initial attack, but badly infected plants should be removed and burned at once.

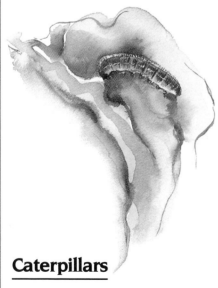

Caterpillars

The larval stage of various moths and butterflies may eat the foliage and flowers of bulbs. Holes are chewed into leaves and flowers, or

DISEASES

Many bulb diseases are fungal, thriving during warm, humid weather or when bulbs are planted in places with poor air circulation, such as badly ventilated greenhouses. Before storing lifted bulbs, dust with fungicide, then place in a single layer on a tray. Alternatively, store bulbs in net bags in an airy place. Bulbs found to be mouldy are best discarded.

Grey mould Botrytis

This arises at any time of year during rainy, humid weather, and especially in very sheltered, still locations.

At first, spots appear on leaves and flowers but these soon grow into a dense grey mould. In greenhouses, improve ventilation and everywhere keep foliage and flowers as dry as possible.

Fusarium

A very serious disease which will spread rapidly if left unchecked, Fusarium is most common during rainy periods in high summer. The first signs of infection are small black spots (the spores of the fungus) which then enter the bulb, causing it to rot. Water run-off and infected soil on your hands, feet or tools will spread the disease. An infected bulb, and those surrounding it, should be dug up and burned. Dip tools used in fungicide solution, light a fire in the hole in which the bulb grew, and keep it burning to sterilise the soil.

Viral diseases

Viral diseases can strike any bulb and there is no cure. Signs of infection include streaked leaves and flowers and/or some deformed leaves and flowers.

Viral diseases are transmitted from one plant to another by sucking insects such as aphids and thrips. Effective pest control is the best way to prevent viral infections. Infected plants should be lifted and burned so as not to provide a source of further infection.

Powdery mildew

Mostly a warm-weather problem, powdery mildew first appears as spots of white powder. These grow fast and soon coalesce until whole leaves are covered. Apply a suitable fungicide at first sight and continue at intervals during the summer and early autumn.

Downy mildew

This is often a problem in early spring or autumn if the weather is showery and humid. The first sign of an attack is the appearance of a downy, white growth on the foliage. Spray with fungicide at first sight.

Bulbs to Plant in Late Winter/Spring

Bulbs in this section are mostly planted at the start of the growing season for flowering in late spring, summer or early autumn. Depending on your climate, some may be planted at other times. If so, this is noted in the "Planting Tips" details of individual entries.

All plant dimensions and planting depths are given in metric and imperial measurements. The conversions have been rounded off to the nearest whole number.

Begonia

Family: *Begoniaceae (Begonia family).* **Type:** *tuber.* **Native to:** *central and South America, tropical and southern Africa and east Asia. Climate varies over this vast area but generally mild to warm year-round with rainy summers and somewhat drier winters. Virtually all tuberous Begonias are hybrids developed from species from many different places, so homeland conditions are less relevant.*

■ **Preferred climate:** cold, cool and frost-free gardens. Possible in cooler, highland areas of the tropics. These summer-growing plants are not for hot, humid places. They do best where summer nights are cool, 16-18°C (61-64°F), and the days mild – around 23°C (73°F).

■ **Planting tips:** plant outdoors in spring when night temperatures remain above 12°C (55°F). Alternatively, start tubers indoors or in a greenhouse in late winter if this night-time temperature can be provided. Plant tubers in gritty, well-drained soil or potting mix that also contains some peat for moisture retention. Tubers should be level with the surface and receive very bright light, but not direct sun. Outdoors, shelter from wind is also essential. Keep soil very lightly moist, gradually giving more water as growth proceeds and the weather warms. In the greenhouse, keep tubers well aired and don't crowd too closely together.

■ **Growing season:** spring, summer and early autumn. Some varieties are erect to about 40cm (16in), others are much smaller, while others still are pendulous.

■ **Flowering season:** in summer and early autumn. Flowers may be single or double, relatively small or the size of a saucer. Colour range includes every shade except blue and green.

■ **Care:** water carefully. Tubers will rot if drainage is poor or if they are over-watered. Avoid wetting the foliage or flowers. Apply a ration of slow-release fertiliser to plants grown in the garden at planting time. In pots, feed fortnightly with a diluted solution of liquid organic fertiliser. Taller, large-flowered hybrids are brittle and will need staking. When temperatures start to fall at summer's end, stop feeding and gradually reduce watering. When leaves yellow, cut them, leaving some stem attached to the tuber and allow the tuber to dry. When dry, stem stubs will snap off easily. Lift, clean and store the tubers in just-moist peat, sphagnum or vermiculite. They will desiccate if stored dry over winter, and rot if too damp. Store over winter at 10°C (50°F).

■ **In pots:** Begonias are ideal pot or basket plants, especially the big-flowered hybrids. They are hard to keep indefinitely in the dry air of indoors; they're better in an airy shade house or conservatory. Don't overpot; these plants prefer their roots to be crowded.

Right: The stunning flowers of tuberous Begonias come in a wide range of colours and sizes. They are among the most spectacular flowers you can grow but do best where summers are relatively cool.

Inset, right: Flowers may be single or double, plain or bicoloured, frilled or picoteed (with a coloured border). This is the hybrid 'Can-Can'.

Inset, far right: Sometimes used in garden beds, tuberous Begonias like these are better suited to pots or baskets.

Brunsvigia

Candelabra lily

Family: *Amaryllidaceae (Hippeastrum family).* **Type:** *bulb.* **Native to:** *inland parts of the eastern Cape Province (South Africa) where summers are hot and dry, and winters frost-free. Rainfall is low and mostly occurs during late autumn and the winter months.*

■ **Preferred climate:** subtropical and frost-free climates that are mostly dry between early spring and late summer. Rain at this time may stop the plant flowering. The bulb is not hardy at all; it's at risk in temperatures below 4°C (39°F).

■ **Planting tips:** plant in spring, with one-third of the bulb remaining above ground. Any well-drained soil suits. The bulbs do not like disturbance of their roots, so site them where they can be left alone. In hot areas, light shade during the afternoon preserves flower colour; elsewhere, grow them in full sun.

■ **Growing season:** late summer to early spring. Leaves low but flower stem rises to around 75cm (2ft 6in).

■ **Flowering season:** late summer. The rosy-pink flowers appear before the leaves.

■ **Care:** apply a light ration of complete plant food when leaves appear. At the cooler limit of their range, a coarse mulch piled up around the bulb in winter will protect it against unexpected lows.

■ **In pots:** Candelabra lily bulbs are the biggest of all – up to 30cm long – so they need to be grown in large tubs where they can be left alone. Tub culture can be successful in a climate where the rainfall pattern is unsuitable. In this case, tubs must be sheltered from rain and exposed to full light.

Below: Brunsvigia josephinae **produces striking, spherical heads of rosy-pink flowers.**

Jack Hobbs

Crinum

Family: *Amaryllidaceae (Hippeastrum family).* **Type:** *bulb.* **Native to:** *tropical and subtropical regions throughout the world where the climate is warm year-round, often with most of the rain during the warmer months.*

■ **Preferred climate:** tropical, subtropical and frost-free gardens. *Crinum powellii* is probably the hardiest of the species, tolerating -5°C (23°F). With the protection of a sunny wall and a thick blanket of mulch, it may even tolerate -10°C (14°F) for a night or two. Other species are not hardy.

■ **Planting tips:** plant in spring or autumn with their necks above soil level in full sun, partial shade or dappled shade. All species prefer deep, acidic, well-drained soils that contain plenty of humus. Crinums are big plants and, while their

flowers are striking, the bulky foliage tends to be straggly and rather unattractive – although very attractive to snails!

■ **Growing season:** spring, summer and early autumn, to at least 1m (3ft) tall, sometimes more, and almost as wide.

■ **Flowering season:** late spring, summer or autumn, depending on the species. Flowers vary from pure white through to shades of pink. Some are fragrant.

■ **Care:** Crinum needs plenty of water during the warmer months, dryness during late autumn and winter. Bait or spray for slugs and snails.

■ **In pots:** possible, but large tubs are necessary as the bulb and the plant are big. Don't repot often as flowering is improved when plant is potbound.

*Above: Crinum powellii **is one of the hardiest species. Its abundant flowers are fragrant.***

Cyrtanthus

Joy Harland/Jack Hobbs

Scarborough lily, George lily, Ifafa lily, Fire lily, Vallota

Family: *Amaryllidaceae (Hippeastrum family).* **Type:** *bulb.* **Native to:** *most species come from the parts of South Africa with summer rainfall. They are widespread from the south-western Cape, along the southern and eastern coasts through Natal and*

Cypella

Family: *Iridaceae (Iris family).*
Type: *bulb.* **Native to:** *Peru, Argentina, Uruguay and Brazil where the climate is mild to warm year-round. Frosts of -10°C (14°F) are possible. Rainfall is fairly evenly distributed throughout the year. The most common species,* **Cypella herbertii** *and* **C. peruviana** *are generally found at altitudes of up to 3000m (1000ft).*

■ **Preferred climate:** highland tropical to cool-climate gardens. Plants will tolerate light frosts only. The summer-growing Cypella can be lifted in autumn and stored above-freezing over winter. Where frosts are light or unknown, bulb can be left in the ground.

■ **Planting tips:** plant summer growers, such as *C. herbertii,* in early spring (or winter in frost-free climates), winter-growing *C. peruviana* in autumn. Plant bulbs in sun, 5-10cm (2-4in) deep and 15cm (6in) apart in average, well-drained garden soil.

■ **Growing season:** winter growers in autumn, winter and early spring; summer growers in spring, summer and early autumn. Plants grow to about 60cm (2ft).

■ **Flowering season:** in summer or late winter, depending on the species. Flowers of all species are multi-coloured.

■ **Care:** moisture during the growing season and an annual application of a complete plant food or slow-release fertiliser is all these easy bulbs need. Where winters are frequently sharply frosty, lift bulbs in autumn and store them above-freezing over winter.

■ **In pots:** in cold climates bulbs can be grown in pots and sheltered in a greenhouse during spells of cool weather. Plant bulbs 3-5cm (1-2in) deep, the same space apart.

Above: Scarborough or George lily, Cyrtanthus elatus, *is an easy and spectacular bulb best suited to warm climates.*

Right: Cypella herbertii *var. brevicristata,* *is an easily grown, unusual, summer-flowering bulb.*

into Transvaal where the climate is frost-free or near frost-free with year-round rain, weighted towards the warmer months. The Cape and southern coast has a Mediterranean climate with most rain falling during the winter months.

■ **Preferred climate:** outside in tropical, subtropical, frost-free and near frost-free areas; elsewhere as a

potted greenhouse plant. Cyrtanthus will usually tolerate the odd night of -5˚C (23˚F) if planted in a sunny, sheltered spot with a blanket of mulch around the bulbs and with overhead protection from evergreen trees or shrubs. The Scarborough lily (*Cyrtanthus elatus* syn. *Vallota speciosa*) is the hardiest of the popularly cultivated types.

■ **Planting tips:** plant spring-flowering species in autumn and late summer; autumn-flowering species in early spring or, in warm climates, in autumn. Average garden soil will do if it drains well. Bulbs should be planted about 5cm (2in) below the surface. Some gardeners prefer to plant the Scarborough lily with its neck above soil level. Full sun or shade in the afternoon is equally suitable; the latter is best where summers are hot.

■ **Growing season:** spring, summer and early autumn. In warm, frost-free climates, some species are only partially deciduous. Height varies according to the species but 30-45cm (12-18in) is typical.

■ **Flowering season:** spring or late summer/early autumn depending on the species. Flowers range from white through to shades of cream, yellow, salmon, pink and orange-scarlet.

■ **Care:** water well during the growing season and feed with a ration of complete plant food when growth begins. Liquid organic fertiliser through the growing season encourages more flowers the next year. A thin mulch of rotted organic matter applied once or twice a year helps to keep humus in the soil. In an area where frosts are likely, don't water at all from mid-autumn until growth begins, and mulch leafless bulbs to protect them from frost. It may be necessary to scrape this away in spring.

■ **In pots:** all species grow well in containers. Plant shallowly and keep dry in winter. In cold places, store the pots dry and above-freezing until spring.

Dahlia

Family: *Asteraceae (Daisy family).*
Type: *tuber.* **Native to:** *highlands of Mexico where the climate is warm to hot year-round. Warmer months are the wettest, the cooler months are dry to nearly dry.*

■ **Preferred climate:** ideal in subtropical and frost-free areas, but it's possible to grow Dahlias anywhere with a growing season of four months or more.

■ **Planting tips:** plant in spring just as frosts (if any) are finishing. Growth buds are clustered around the stem ends of tubers. Each tuber must have at least one "eye" and a sliver of last year's stem attached. Plant so that the eyes are 8-15cm (3-6in) below the surface in deeply dug, fairly rich, well-drained soil. Tall-growing types will need staking. Place stake at planting time with a maximum of three tubers around it. Dahlias must have full sun.

■ **Growing season:** spring, summer and early autumn. Tree Dahlias reach 3-4m (10-13ft), dwarf Dahlias only 30-45cm (12-18in). There are many sizes in between.

■ **Flowering season:** late spring, summer and autumn. Where summers are hot, flowers of tubers planted in early spring can be bleached and short-lived. It's often better to delay planting until late spring so that flowers appear in autumn.

■ **Care:** dig planting site deeply and incorporate plenty of rotted manure or compost and a ration of complete plant food. Keep site lightly moist until growth begins, then, as the warmth and plant growth increase, gradually water more. Feed periodically and pinch out growing tips of tall types two or three times while they are young. This makes the plant bushier and it will ultimately yield more flowers. As autumn progresses, the foliage will wither. After the first frost, or by the end of autumn, lift the tubers, clean, label and store them above-freezing until planting time in the following spring.

■ **In pots:** dwarf and annual varieties are suitable for potting.

Right: Spectacular when grouped together, Dahlias may be dwarf, medium or tall plants. There are at least 11 flower shapes to choose from and all colours are available except blue and green.

Below, from left: A semi-cactus Dahlia variety; cactus Dahlia 'Cristy'; orchid-flowered Dahlia 'Jescot Julie'; Collarette Dahlia 'Claire de Lune'.

Geoffrey Burnie/Lorna Rose/Photos Horticultural

Dierama

Wand flower, Fairy wand, Fairy bells, Fairy fishing rod, Angel's fishing rod

Family: *Iridaceae (Iris family).*
Type: *corm.* **Native to:** *South Africa in moist grassland between 1000-3000m (3300-10,000ft) where rain occurs throughout the year but most falls during the warmer months. Winter nights can be sharply frosty.*

■ **Preferred climate:** suits cool and frost-free areas. Plants will tolerate -18°C (0°F) but do better where temperatures don't fall below -10°C (14°F). Can be grown in pots in a cool greenhouse.

■ **Planting tips:** plant in spring or early autumn when frosts are finished, 8-13cm (3-5in) deep and at least 30cm (12in) apart. Plants enjoy humus-rich soil that is constantly moist but not boggy. Full sun or dappled shade suits, the latter where summers are very hot.

■ **Growing season:** plants are evergreen but grow most strongly during spring and summer. Clumps of grassy foliage can reach 1m (3ft); flowers above this.

■ **Flowering season:** in summer or autumn, earliest where winters are mild, in rosy-purple, pink or white.

■ **Care:** can be kept very slightly moist in winter. Water freely during spring and summer. After blooming, mulch plants with rotted organic matter. Tidy plants in winter by removing dead and dying leaves. If necessary, apply complete plant food or slow-release fertiliser once each spring or mulch with rotted manure.

■ **In pots:** good in tall pots or urns placed where the plant's graceful, spreading habit is not confined. Waterproof rather than porous pots are best.

Eucharis

Amazon lily, Eucharist lily

Family: *Amaryllidaceae (Hippeastrum family).* **Type:** *bulb.*
Native to: *Colombia and tropical forests and rainforests in adjacent countries where the climate is hot, humid and rainy year-round or with a dry season in winter.*

■ **Preferred climate:** humid, tropical and subtropical areas as a year-round garden or pot plant. Grow in a heated greenhouse in cool or cold places. In this instance, they will need winter night temperatures above 10°C (50°F) and high humidity.

■ **Planting tips:** plant in spring in friable, fertile soil that contains rotted organic matter. Plants will grow outdoors in non-tropical, humid, frost-free places. Site in the warmest spot possible. They will tolerate full sun in winter and the cooler halves of autumn and spring,

but prefer some shade during the middle hours of the day at other times. In the tropics they will accept dappled or full shade year-round. Once planted, don't disturb for years. In the greenhouse, start bulbs at about 21°C (70°F). As growth proceeds keep humidity high and raise the temperature to about 27°C (80°F) in summer.

■ **Growing season:** plants are evergreen and grow year-round in rainy, tropical areas or a heated greenhouse. In monsoonal tropics and frost-free subtropical and temperate places, plants lose some leaves and go slow during autumn, winter and early spring.

■ **Flowering season:** in the rainy tropics and greenhouses, Eucharis produces flushes of flowers throughout the year but flowers most heavily in late autumn and winter. Elsewhere, flowers appear in spring and autumn. They are white and fragrant.

■ **Care:** protect from snails and slugs. Never let them dry out but, during the cooler months, less water can be given. In the greenhouse, the temperature can be gradually reduced to a winter night minimum of 10°C (50°F). Reduce watering at the same time and do not feed. Feed with liquid organic fertiliser during spring and summer only.

■ **In pots:** plant about 3cm (1in) apart with neck and shoulders of each bulb above soil level. Eucharis like to be potbound. As the flowers are heavy and downward pointing, hanging baskets can give the best view of the flowers.

*Above: Fairy fishing rods, Dierama pulcherrimum, **make elegant, pendulous clumps.***

*Right: Eucharis grandiflora **produces flushes of pretty, daffodil-like flowers right through the year.***

Gloriosa

Family: *Colchicaceae (Colchicum family).* **Type:** *tuber.* **Native to:** *eastern South Africa, tropical Africa, India where winters are dry and vary from near frost-free to warm. Summers are always hot and humid with plenty of rain.*

■ **Preferred climate:** tropical, subtropical, frost-free and near frost-free gardens. Plants are winter-dormant and, when heavily mulched, can tolerate frosts as low as -10°C (14°F) if they are not frequent enough to freeze the soil. Gloriosa does better where there are no frosts. They may be grown in containers in cold climates and kept dry through the winter, at above-freezing temperatures. When growth begins in spring, keep them in a greenhouse with night temperatures above 15°C (59°F) until outside night temperatures remain at that level.

■ **Planting tips:** plant in warm climates, anytime from autumn to early spring or after frosts in cooler areas. Plant horizontally, 10cm (4in) deep in fertile, well-drained soil. Place near a support, such as a trellis, or under an open-foliaged shrub through which the plant can climb. Plants must be able to grow into full sun and will scramble through low shrubs.

■ **Growing season:** spring, summer and early autumn to 1.5-2m (5-7ft), climbing by means of tendrils at the point of each leaf.

■ **Flowering season:** late spring to summer in warm climates, mid to late summer and early autumn in cooler climates. Flowers are red and yellow, with or without wavy edges to the petals.

■ **Care:** Gloriosa demand plenty of water during the growing season but can dry out at the end of summer. If left in the ground, a mulch of rotted manure and compost, applied in autumn, is enough feeding. Tubers prefer dryness over winter. They may rot in heavy soils in regions of winter

Lorna Rose

rainfall, but will accept moderate winter rain if drainage is good. In colder areas, lift, clean and store tubers well above freezing during autumn and winter.

■ **In pots:** plant three tubers per 25cm (10in) pot, or one per 15cm (6in) pot. Where summer night temperatures don't stay above 15˚C (59˚F) for long, start the tubers indoors in late winter on a sunny windowsill in a warm room (or in a heated greenhouse). Pot up as plants grow, then transfer to the garden when night temperatures reach 15˚C (59˚F). For permanent pot culture, a slender stake at least 1m (3ft) long will be necessary.

Hymenocallis

Spider lily, Summer daffodil

Family: *Amaryllidaceae (Hippeastrum family).* **Type:** *bulb.* **Native to:** *southern USA through Central America and West Indies to northern South America where the climate is warm to hot year-round. Winters frost-free or nearly frost-free. Rain can fall year-round or winters may be dry.*

■ **Preferred climate:** Tropical, subtropical, frost-free and near frost-free gardens. The winter-dormant types will tolerate -2˚C (28˚F) if protected with a mulch of straw or fern fronds and the soil is barely moist. They are from areas where winters are relatively dry.

■ **Planting tips:** plant deciduous (winter-dormant) species in early spring; evergreen species when available. Plant 8-15cm (3-6in) deep and about 25cm (10in) or more apart – they become quite big plants. All species need good drainage and enjoy a fertile, humus-enriched soil. They will accept full sun or part shade.

■ **Growing season:** deciduous types grow from spring through the autumn; evergreens will grow

year-round; however they are least active during the winter.

■ **Flowering season:** all species flower during summer with white or cream blossoms. Many are fragrant.

■ **Care:** evergreen species need water year-round but the deciduous types prefer a fairly dry winter. Where winters are wet or a little too cool, lift the bulbs in autumn and store them dry above-freezing until the following spring. If soil is rich in rotted organic matter, no additional feeding is necessary. In good conditions, these bulbs multiply fast and need division every three years.

■ **In pots:** possible in fairly big tubs but Hymenocallis are better garden plants.

Left: The exotic Gloriosa superba *is one of the few climbing bulbs. It looks terrific when allowed to scramble through open shrubs.*

Above: Elegant and evergreen, Hymenocallis littoralis **needs a frost-free, subtropical climate to do well. Flowers are fragrant.**

Sandersonia

Christmas bells, Chinese lantern

Family: *Colchicaceae (Colchicum family)*. **Type:** *tuber.* **Native to:** *eastern South Africa where the climate is warm, subtropical with some rain all year but most falling during the warmer months. Frosts are light or unknown.*

■ **Preferred climate:** tropical, subtropical and frost-free gardens. Can be grown in cooler climates where there is a frost-free growing season of six months or more. In even colder climates, grow in pots kept in a greenhouse when frosts are likely.

■ **Planting tips:** plant in frost-free climates in late winter or early spring. In colder climates, plant out when frosts are nearly finished or in pots in a heated greenhouse from late winter onwards. Plant tubers 8-10cm (3-4in) deep, 25cm (10in) apart in deep, well-drained soil that contains rotted organic matter. Dig the soil deeply before planting as this will help the roots to penetrate. Since the stems tend to be thin, they will need the support of a stake or trellis. Where summers are hot, plants accept

dappled midday and afternoon shade; elsewhere full sun is best for them.

■ **Growing season:** spring, summer and early autumn on semi-erect stems to 1m (3ft) tall.

■ **Flowering season:** from mid-spring to early summer, a little later in cooler climates. The small flowers are orange-yellow. Stems last well when cut.

■ **Care:** water from the time growth appears, gradually giving more water as growth proceeds and summer approaches. After blooming, reduce watering in stages. Plants will begin to die back in autumn and need to be kept as dry as possible until the following spring. Where winters are wet, lift tubers and store dry through winter. Apply a ration of complete plant food or slow-release fertiliser when growth begins.

■ **In pots:** Christmas bells make excellent pot plants but use the deepest possible containers and insert a stake at planting time. Plant tubers more shallowly in pots.

Scadoxus

Paint brush, Blood lily, Snake lily

Family: *Amaryllidaceae (Hippeastrum family)*. **Type:** *bulb.* **Native to:** *southern and eastern South Africa and tropical Africa where the climate is warm to hot year-round with rain evenly distributed or mostly in summer. Frosts of -10°C (14°F) are possible inland but these are not common or prolonged. Winter days are sunny and above 10°C (50°F).*

■ **Preferred climate:** tropical, subtropical, frost-free and near frost-free gardens. In colder areas, grow summer-growing species in pots brought undercover and kept above freezing while dormant in autumn and winter. Evergreen species will tolerate light frosts only.

■ **Planting tips:** plant in winter (in frost-free areas) or spring in well-drained soil that contains

plenty of rotted organic matter. Place bulbs with their necks at soil level. While plants will tolerate full sun, a site that receives some shade during the afternoon is preferred. The big and impressive *Scadoxus multiflorus* subsp. *katharinae* will flower in full shade.

■ **Growing season:** spring to autumn. Evergreen species grow year-round, but are least active in winter. Plants range in height, *S. multiflorus* subsp. *katharinae* being the biggest with a mature height of more than 1m (3ft) possible. A more usual height would be 50cm (20in).

■ **Flowering season:** late winter to early autumn depending on the species and your climate – the cooler the climate, the later the flowers appear. Flowers may be salmon pink or orange-red.

■ **Care:** water whenever leaves are present if rain does not fall. No feeding is necessary if soil is rich in humus. Stop watering when leaves begin to wither in autumn. In cool climates keep dry, above freezing in winter. In frost-free and warmer gardens, moderate winter rain is harmless if soil drains fast. Once planted, do not lift bulbs frequently.

■ **In pots:** Scadoxus make striking and unusual pot plants; use a wide tub for the best display. Plants can be overwintered dry in their containers. Pot culture is essential where winters are cool and wet.

*Left: Christmas bells, Sandersonia aurantiaca, **make unusual additions to summer flower arrangements. They are easy to grow if given a dry winter.***

*Inset, left: Scadoxus puniceus **shoot straight from the ground in late winter or early spring.***

*Inset, right: the flowers of Scadoxus puniceus **make a dramatic display. Leaves follow soon after.***

Schizostylis

Crimson flag, River lily

Family: *Iridaceae (Iris family).*
Type: *rhizome.* **Native to:** *eastern South Africa and tropical Africa where winters vary from sharply frosty in the highlands to frost-free nearer the coast. Winter days are warm and sunny. Rain falls in every month but, over much of the range, most falls in late spring and summer.*

■ **Preferred climate:** cool, frost-free and subtropical gardens. Plants will accept -10˚C (14˚F), which is very low in their native ranges, but not frequently and not for long periods. In cold climates, they can be grown in pots and given greenhouse protection until outside conditions are mild. Maintain winter nights above freezing, days about 10˚C (50˚F).

■ **Planting tips:** plant in late winter or early spring, 8cm (3in) deep and 15cm (6in) apart in humus-rich, moisture-retentive soil that drains enough to prevent sogginess. In the wild, plants are found on stream banks which have constant access to water. In gardens, they do best in a moist spot. The best aspect is full sun, although a little light shade or an hour or two of full shade in a day is tolerable.

■ **Growing season:** spring, summer and autumn to a height of about 60cm (2ft). Plants spread to form thick, grassy clumps.

■ **Flowering season:** late summer and autumn in scarlet or shades of pink. Named hybrids, with more and bigger flowers than the species, are available.

■ **Care:** plenty of water is their main need; plants are most successful where summers include frequent showers and are not too hot. If soil is rich in humus, no additional feeding is necessary. In good conditions, plants multiply fast and clumps should be divided every 2-3 years in late winter. Flowers may not appear the first summer after a division.

Below: Permanently moist soil beside a pond is ideal for the lively, water-loving river lily, Schizostylis coccinea.

Right: Schizostylis 'Jennifer' is a pretty pink-flowered hybrid.

Nancy Gardiner / Photos Horticultural

Sprekelia

Jacobean lily, Aztec lily, St James lily

Family: *Amaryllidaceae (Hippeastrum family).* **Type:** *bulb.* **Native to:** *Mexico where the climate is warm to hot year-round. Winters may be lightly frosty – plants have no trouble with -7°C (45°F) – and relatively dry.*

■ **Preferred climate:** subtropical, frost-free and near frost-free gardens. In colder climates grow them in pots overwintered above freezing.

■ **Planting tips:** plant in late winter or early spring with the tip of the bulb just poking above the surface. Soil should be well drained and of average fertility. A site in full sun is always best.

■ **Growing season:** spring to early autumn except in frost-free areas with year-round rain. In such climates, it keeps some of its leaves all year. Plants grow to a height of about 30cm (12in).

■ **Flowering season:** mid to late spring, with odd flowers through summer and autumn in rainy, frost-free areas.

■ **Care:** water lightly when flowers first emerge, gradually giving more water as leaves grow and summer approaches. At the end of summer, if leaves begin to yellow, reduce water. In their natural range, plants become dormant in the dry season, from the end of summer to early spring. Where winters are barely frosty or warmer, cool-season rain is harmless if bulbs are planted in well-drained soil. If feeding is necessary, apply complete plant food after flowers fade.

■ **In pots:** Jacobean lilies make very showy pot plants which enjoy being crowded together. Withhold water from early autumn to enforce dormancy. Store bulbs in pots at above-freezing but do not let them dry out for long periods; a little moisture is needed during their dormant period.

Tigridia

Jockey's cap lily, Tiger flower

Family: *Iridaceae (Iris family).* **Type:** *corm.* **Native to:** *Mexico and Guatemala where the climate is warm to hot year-round with a dry season in winter. Frosts of up to -10°C (14°F) are possible but not common or prolonged.*

■ **Preferred climate:** cool, frost-free and subtropical gardens. Plants are not cold-hardy but are summer-growing, winter-dormant, so they can be lifted in autumn where winters are too cold for them.

■ **Planting tips:** plant in early spring (after frosts if any), 8cm (3in) deep and 20cm (8in) apart in friable, well-drained soil in full sun.

■ **Growing season:** spring, summer and early autumn to a height of about 50cm (20in).

■ **Flowering season:** late spring or early summer. Stems produce a long succession of brightly coloured blooms that each last one day.

■ **Care:** plenty of water during the growing season and a mulch of rotted manure over the plants when dormant is about all that's needed. Plants may lose vigour after a few years but healthy new stock is easily raised from seed saved from the previous year and sown in spring. Where winters are sharply frosty, lift bulbs when foliage withers in autumn, clean and dry them, then store above 10°C (50°F).

■ **In pots:** pot shallowly into deep containers of good-quality potting mix to which has been added a ration of slow-release fertiliser.

Above: Curiously attractive, the Aztec lily, Sprekelia formosissima, *is always a striking addition to a garden.*

Right: With their spotted centres and bright petals, Tigridia pavonia *are some of summer's most eye-catching bulbs.*

Tropaeolum

Nasturtium

Family: *Tropaeolaceae (Nasturtium family).* **Type:** *tuber.* **Native to:** *southern Chile where the climate is cool to mild year-round with rainy summers and winters that are usually moderately frosty. Frequent fogs are a feature of the moist Chilean coast.*

■ **Preferred climate:** cool and near frost-free gardens. Plants are hardy to -15°C (5°F) and thrive in areas with cool, moist summers. They are not successful where summers are hot and humid or hot and dry.

■ **Planting tips:** plant in spring, 10cm (4in) deep in well-drained soil made moisture-retentive with the addition of compost or rotted manure. Take care handling the brittle tubers and try to site them so that the root zone will remain shaded while the upper parts can reach the sun.

■ **Growing season:** spring, summer and early autumn to a height of about 5m (17ft).

Jerry Harpur / Jack Hobbs

Zephyranthes

Rain lily, Zephyr lily, Fairy lily

Family: *Amaryllidaceae (Hippeastrum family).* **Type:** *bulb.* **Native to:** *south-eastern USA, West Indies, Mexico, Guatemala and Guyana where the climate is warm to hot and humid year-round. Light frosts are possible inland. Rain falls every month or there may be a dry season in winter.*

■ **Preferred climate:** cool, frost-free and subtropical gardens. They can be grown in pots in colder areas if given greenhouse protection when temperatures fall below freezing.

■ **Planting tips:** plant in spring when frosts, if any, have gone. Plant 5cm (2in) deep, the same distance apart, in good-quality soil in full sun.

■ **Growing season:** spring and summer or, in the case of evergreen species, year-round. All species are low, rarely exceeding 25cm (10in). Over time they spread to form dense clumps.

■ **Flowering season:** most species flower in late summer or early autumn. Flowers may be white, cream, pink or yellow, depending on the species.

■ **Care:** keep moist always, increasing water during spring and summer, decreasing it in autumn and winter. Even deciduous types need some water when dormant. In cold climates, lift bulbs in autumn and store above-freezing until the following spring.

■ **In pots:** excellent pot plants, especially in wide, shallow containers. Use a peaty potting mix and feed monthly during the growing season with liquid organic fertiliser.

Left: The eye-catching flame nasturtium, Tropaeolum speciosum, *is one of several tuberous, climbing nasturtiums suitable for areas with cool, moist summers.*

Inset left: The sprightly rain lily, Zephyranthes candida, *is perhaps the hardiest species and the most common. Its brilliant white flowers appear in early autumn.*

Above: Other Zephyranthes species have pink or yellow flowers. This is a rare yellow form of the usually pink Z. macrosiphon.

■ **Flowering season:** from late spring through the summer.

■ **Care:** ensure soil is moist at planting time and remains so until shoots appear. Water more generously as growth and the season progresses. Well-established plants can tolerate dryness but always look and flower best when water is freely available. In early autumn, the vine will begin to yellow and die back. If winters are very cold, cover the root zone with a thick layer of mulch, scraping back to a more shallow layer before new growth emerges in spring.

■ **In pots:** possible in big tubs set next to a trellis for support. In containers, attention to watering is critical, especially in high summer. Don't place where the pot will receive full sun.

Bulbs to Plant in
Late Spring/Summer

Bulbs in this section are planted when the weather is warm to hot, because they are either frost-tender,

summer growers or summer-dormant bulbs that grow in autumn and winter.

All plant dimensions and planting depths are given in metric and imperial measurements. The conversions have been rounded off to the nearest whole number.

Achimenes

Orchid pansy, Nut orchid, Mother's tears, Widow's tears, Magic flower, Hot water plant

Family: *Gesneriaceae (African violet family).* **Type:** *rhizome.* **Native to:** *central and northern South America where the climate is tropical or subtropical with dry winters.*

■ **Preferred climate:** tropical, subtropical and frost-free areas as a year-round garden, pot or basket plant. It is a greenhouse plant only in the UK, Canada and other places with cool summer nights. Temperatures below 15°C (59°F) stop growth and send the plant into dormancy.

■ **Planting tips:** plant outside when night temperatures always exceed 15°C (59°F) or in spring in a heated greenhouse 3cm (1in) deep in well-drained potting mix or light soil that is rich in rotted organic matter. Keep lightly moist only until shoots appear. The plant likes morning sun or dappled shade, not hot midday or afternoon sun.

■ **Growing season:** spring, summer and early autumn, to 60cm (2ft) tall and wide in the tropics, about 20-30cm (8-12in) elsewhere.

■ **Flowering season:** summer in purple, mauve, pink, white or yellow.

■ **Care:** keep evenly moist and feed when growing and flowering. Pinch-prune young shoots to induce bushiness and more flowers. Stop feeding and begin to dry out in autumn. Where winters are always frost-free, rhizomes can be left in the ground and will not be harmed by winter rain if the soil is well drained. Elsewhere, store dry rhizomes above 7°C (45°F).

■ **In pots:** don't overcrowd, always use tepid water – over 15°C (59°F) – and keep pots evenly moist. Coolness and/or dryness will induce dormancy. In mid-autumn, leave the plant to dry out.

Left: Summer-growing Achimenes are vibrant little plants in the garden, in pots or baskets. Where temperatures do not remain above 15°C (59°F) for at least three months, they will need greenhouse protection.

Photos Horticultural / Geoffrey Burnie

Amaryllis

Belladonna lily, Jersey lily, Naked lady

Family: *Amaryllidaceae (Hippeastrum family).* **Type:** *bulb.* **Native to:** *coast and inland parts of south-western Cape Province (South Africa) where there is a Mediterranean climate.*

■ **Preferred climate:** subtropical, frost-free and near frost-free. They tolerate winter nights down to -5°C (23°F) with little or no damage to foliage. Plants will live through the odd -12°C (10°F) if planted 15-20cm (6-8in) deep and mulched, but the foliage will be damaged and the plant will suffer a set back.

■ **Planting tips:** plant in late spring or summer. In frost-free gardens, plant with the neck of the bulb at soil level. In colder places, plant up to 20cm (8in) deep. Sandy soil containing organic matter is best, but average garden soil will do if it drains freely. Plants grow in full sun, part-shade or dappled shade, the latter only in hot climates.

■ **Growing season:** autumn, winter and spring; it is dormant in summer. Foliage is a clump of straps about 30cm (12in) tall.

■ **Flowering season:** late summer, early autumn. Flowers appear straight out of the ground on leafless stems. Flowers are usually soft pink but may be rosy-mauve or white, are sweetly fragrant and make impressive cut flowers. When flowers have faded, leaves follow.

■ **Care:** water as soon as flower spikes appear and keep moist until foliage fades the following summer. If desired, scratch in a ration of complete plant food or slow-release fertiliser when leaves appear. Once planted, leave alone for years as disturbed bulbs may take two or three years to reflower.

■ **In pots:** bulbs are big and three would need a tub 35cm (14in) across. Use a very well-drained potting mix. Do not expect flowers in the first year.

Above: Stately Belladonna lilies, Amaryllis belladonna, **come in a range of soft or deep pinks and white. They are sweetly fragrant.**

Inset, above: Flower stems shoot straight out of the ground in late summer or early autumn.

Caladium

Angel wings, Elephant's ears

Family: *Araceae (Arum lily family).*
Native to: *Brazil in tropical rainforest with heat, rain and high humidity year-round.*

■ **Preferred climate:** outdoors in tropical and subtropical areas only. Greenhouse, conservatory or indoor pot plant elsewhere.

■ **Planting tips:** in cool climates, start tubers indoors in late spring by just covering with a moist, peaty potting mix at 22°C (72°F). When shoots appear, give very bright but indirect light and a little more heat. If night temperatures always remain above 16°C (61°F), plants may be transferred to a sheltered, warm but shady spot outside. The minimum night temperature tolerated by equatorial plants is 16°C (61°F). Below that, leaves will begin to deteriorate and the tuber will become dormant.

■ **Growing season:** late spring and summer out of the tropics, year-round in humid, tropical climates. Well-grown plants may reach a height of 75cm (2ft 6in).

■ **Flowering season:** flowers are insignificant; plants are grown for their brilliantly coloured and patterned leaves.

■ **Care:** keep warm, moist and humid while growing. In pots, feed with liquid or soluble plant food once a month. When leaves begin to deteriorate, gradually reduce heat and watering until dry. Lift and clean tubers at 10-12°C (50-54°F). Store over winter at, or above, 12°C (54°F) in just moist sphagnum or peat.

■ **In pots:** is the usual way to grow Caladium out of the tropics. Use one tuber per 15cm (6in) pot.

Lorna Rose / Murray Fagg Australian National Botanic Gardens

Calostemma

Garland lily, Crown lily

Family: *Amaryllidaceae (Hippeastrum family).* **Type**: *bulb.* **Native to:** *northern, eastern and south-eastern Australia where the climate varies. In the north it is monsoonal tropical with dry winters. In the rest of the habitat it is mild to warm, generally dry with rain most likely in the cooler months.*

■ **Preferred climate:** outside in subtropical, frost-free and near frost-free areas; in pots under glass and with winter heat where temperatures routinely fall below -5°C (23°F).

■ **Planting tips:** plant in early summer in full sun or bright, lightly dappled shade. Soil must be very well-drained but not overly sandy and bulbs should be planted so that their necks protrude above soil level. If water is necessary, apply only when plants are in leaf. Bulbs are very drought-tolerant, so they will usually live on rain alone. Calostemma bulbs look best when they are planted in a large drift.

■ **Growing season:** during the cooler months, to maximum height of about 50cm (20in).

■ **Flowering season:** spring or early autumn, depending on the species. Flowers are white, yellow or rosy pink.

■ **Care:** very little is needed. Where frosts are likely, grow against a sunny wall or large rock. A dry rest during late spring and summer is essential for good flowering, so do not site with other plants that need water during this time. When growth begins, lightly dig in a complete plant food or slow-release fertiliser.

■ **In pots:** good in pots, especially wide dishes where a massed display can be achieved. Add some coarse sand or fine gravel to ensure potting mix is well drained. Bulbs can be stored dry in their containers.

Left: Exotic with decorative leaves, Caladiums are usually sold as indoor plants. If you have four months when temperatures never fall below 16°C (61°F), you can enjoy them outdoors.

Inset, above left and right: Garland lilies are one of the few bulbs native to Australia and, while they are not particularly showy as individuals, they are impressive in a mass planting. The yellow form is Calostemma luteum, **the purple** Calostemma purpureum.

Polyxena

Family: *Liliaceae (Lily family).*
Type: *bulb.* **Native to:** *west coast of South Africa to the eastern Cape where the climate is a Mediterranean type with wet winters and hot, dry, or relatively dry, summers. Frosts are light or unknown.*

■ **Preferred climate:** subtropical and frost-free gardens, especially those with a Mediterranean climate. In colder areas, grow it in a container under glass. The bulbs are winter-growing and intolerant of all but the lightest of frosts.

■ **Planting tips:** plant in summer, just below the surface and closely spaced for the best display. Plants demand good drainage and do best in gravelly or sandy soil in full sun. They are small plants,

well-suited to rockeries or similar raised beds or troughs in which alpines are often grown.

■ **Growing season:** autumn and winter to a height of about 10cm (4in).

■ **Flowering season:** late autumn or early winter. They come with pink, white or mauve flowers. The flowers are short-lived but, if you plant a number of bulbs closely together, you can achieve a successful display.

■ **Care:** plant in moist soil, or water once planted. Do not water again until growth begins. Then, keep moist until foliage begins to wither. The bulbs will tolerate total dryness while dormant. In frost-free areas, bulbs planted in the ground will accept moderate summer rain

where the soil is very well drained. They will rot in prolonged rainy, humid weather. Protect from snails.

■ **In pots:** ideal in wide, shallow containers which can be sheltered from summer rain and brought indoors when plant is in bloom.

Above: Unusual looking and delicate, Polyxena ensifolia has pink, white or mauve flowers that are sweetly scented.

Right: Polyxena corymbosa has beautiful, unscented pink flowers and gives a good display in pots.

Worsleya

Blue Amaryllis, Empress of Brazil

Family: *Amaryllidaceae (Hippeastrum family).* **Type:** *bulb.* **Native to:** *southern Brazil where the climate is warm to hot and very humid year-round. Rain falls in every month but summers are wetter than winters.*

■ **Preferred climate:** tropical and subtropical gardens but needs the constant warmth and humidity of a heated greenhouse elsewhere.

■ **Planting tips:** plant in summer in coarse, free-draining soil that contains rotted organic matter. Place the bulb so that the top half or more is out of the ground in a spot that receives full sun. In its native land, this bulb can be seen hanging from cliffs, often within reach of the spray from waterfalls.

■ **Growing season:** year-round but most vigorous during the warmer months. Plants are large and leafy.

■ **Flowering season:** in late spring or summer. The magnificent lilac-blue flowers are big, impressive and long lasting.

■ **Care:** keep moist always but give most water between mid-spring and the end of summer. Feed frequently with a diluted solution of liquid organic fertiliser, but only during the warmer months. In tropical and subtropical gardens, place plants near an irrigation system spray and mist frequently.

■ **In pots:** possibly the best way to grow them, even in tropical areas. Use a very coarse potting mix. In frost-free areas out of the tropics and cooler places, maintain a winter night temperature of 16°C (61°F), raised to 21°C (70°F) in the day. In summer, raise day temperatures to 27°C (80°F) and don't let night temperatures fall below 18°C (65°F). Repot when root bound.

Below: The magnificent, big, blue Amaryllis, Worsleya rayneri, ***is a tropical bulb. Out of the tropics, it is only for enthusiastic greenhouse owners.***

Jack Hobbs

A Seasonal Guide

THE BULB-GROWER'S CALENDAR

*As the three months which make up each season are different in the two hemispheres, we have labelled them
early, mid and late. Early corresponds to the first month of the season, mid to the second, late to the third.
Events have been attributed to a time period based on a general view of the different climates in which we live.
They may not be exact everywhere; gardening does not depend on split-second timing and this calendar
merely gives you a guide that you can refine, using your own local experience.*

SPRING

*September, October, November (southern hemisphere)
March, April, May (northern hemisphere)*

Early spring

In bloom: Anemone,
Anomatheca, Baeometra,
Colchicum, Crocus, Cyclamen,
Cyrtanthus, Eranthis, Erythronium,
Ferraria, Freesia, Fritillaria,
Galanthus, Hippeastrum,
Hyacinthoides, Hyacinthus, Ipheion,
Ixia, Lachenalia, Leopoldia,
Leucocoryne, Muscari, Narcissus,
Ornithogalum, Oxalis, Puschkinia,
Ranunculus, Romulea, Scadoxus,
Scilla, Sternbergia, Tecophilaea,
Tritonia, Tulipa, Veltheimia,
Watsonia, Wurmbea, Zantedeschia.

Plant: summer-growing bulbs two
to three weeks before last frost.

Mulch: cover newly planted bulbs
with mulch to feed and improve soil
texture; it also conserves soil moisture.

Feed: bulbs that are in bloom, or
about to, with liquid or soluble fertiliser.

Mid-spring

In bloom: Allium, Babiana,
Anomatheca, Calostemma,
Camassia, Crocus, Erythronium,
Ferraria, Freesia, Fritillaria,
Hyacinthoides, Hyacinthus, Ipheion,
Ixia, Leopoldia, Leucocoryne,
Muscari, Narcissus, Ornithogalum,
Oxalis, Puschkinia, Romulea,
Sandersonia, Scadoxus, Scilla,
Spiloxene, Sprekelia, Synnotia,
Tecophilaea, Trillium, Tritonia,
Tulipa, Watsonia, Zantedeschia.

Plant: summer-growing bulbs.

Deadhead: remove flowers
when they fade from spring bulbs.
This prevents the bulb from wasting
energy on unwanted seed
production. Leave the stem as
this helps to feed the bulb.

Pest watch: slugs and snails build
up fast in spring, especially if it is
wet. Lay snail pellets or spray
foliage with soluble snail bait.

In greenhouses: empty and
clean greenhouses. Inspect pots and
benches for pest infestations.

Watering: reduce water given to
spring bulbs as their leaves begin to
wither. Do not remove leaves until
they have turned yellow.

Feed: feed summer-growing bulbs
with liquid or soluble fertiliser when
the first signs of growth are seen.

Late spring

In bloom: Allium, Calostemma,
Camassia, Crinum, Dahlia,
Erythronium, Eucharis, Gloriosa,

Freesia, Fritillaria, Ipheion, Ixia, Leucocoryne, Narcissus, Ornithogalum, Ranunculus, Rhodohypoxis, Romulea, Sandersonia, Scadoxus, Scilla, Spiloxene, Sprekelia, Synnotia, Tecophilaea, Tigridia, Trillium, Triteleia, Tritonia, Tropaeolum, Watsonia, Worsleya, Zantedeschia.

Lift: summer-dormant bulbs where summers are wet. Lift tulips and hyacinths when foliage has yellowed. Clean all lifted bulbs, inspect for signs of damage or disease and discard any that are affected. Store in a dark, airy, cool place.

Pest watch: watch for aphids, thrips and mites. The latter multiply fast in warm, dry weather. Control them at first sign of infestation.

Watering: ensure that summer-growing bulbs are kept moist. Many species require generous watering in the early stages of growth. Potted bulbs in sun may dry out fast. Check daily if the weather is warm and dry. Allow summer-dormant bulbs that are left in the ground to dry out.

Stake: tie Dahlias, tall lilies, Gloriosas, Sandersonias and other tall growers to stakes as they grow.

In greenhouses: where summers are hot, whitewash greenhouses or cover with shadecloth to keep cool.

SUMMER

December, January, February (southern hemisphere)
June, July, August (northern hemisphere)

Early summer

In bloom: Achimenes, Allium, Begonia, Calostemma, Camassia, Crinum, Dahlia, Dierama, Eucomis, Galtonia, Gloriosa, Habranthus, Hymenocallis, Ixia, Moraea, Ornithogalum, Oxalis, Rhodohypoxis, Rhodophiala, Romulea, Sandersonia, Scadoxus, Scilla, Tigridia, Trillium, Tritonia, Triteleia, Tropaeolum, Worsleya, Zantedeschia.

Plant: tropical and summer-dormant bulbs.

Feed: feed summer-growing bulbs with liquid or soluble fertiliser.

Weed: clear weeds around bulbs; they compete for water, food and light and can harbour pests.

In greenhouses: ensure ventilation is adequate. Excessive heat and humidity damages plants and encourages fungal diseases.

Mid-summer

In bloom: Achimenes, Allium, Begonia, Crinum, Dahlia, Dierama, Eucomis, Galtonia, Gloriosa, Habranthus, Hymenocallis, Moraea, Ornithogalum, Rhodophiala, Sandersonia, Scadoxus, Scilla, Tritonia, Tropaeolum, Worsleya, Zantedeschia.

Inspect: check stored bulbs for pest infestation, disease or mould; discard any that are affected. Derris dust will help preserve stored bulbs.

Deadhead: remove flowers as they fade, unless seeds are wanted.

Mulch: mulch around bulbs after watering deeply.

In greenhouses: on hot days, wet the floors and benches and mist all foliage to cool and humidify the air. In cold climates, reduce water given to potted Hippeastrums to induce dormancy.

Lift: lift dormant, spring-flowering bulbs that have become over-crowded. Separate and clean the bulbs, retaining only the biggest and healthiest for replanting. Either replant immediately into refurbished soil or store the bulbs until autumn.

Late summer

In bloom: Achimenes, Allium, Amaryllis, Begonia, Brunsvigia, Crinum, Crocosmia, Crocus, Dahlia, Dierama, Eucomis, Habranthus, Hymenocallis, Lycoris, Nerine, Rhodophiala, Scadoxus, Schizostylis, Scilla, Tritonia, Tropaeolum, Watsonia, Wurmbea, Zantedeschia.

Water: reduce water to summer-growing bulbs as flowers finish.

Prepare: dig over and improve soil in preparation for new plantings in autumn. Compost or rotted manure and a ration of complete plant food are good additives.

AUTUMN

March, April, May (southern hemisphere)
September, October, November (northern hemisphere)

Early autumn

In bloom: Amaryllis, Begonia, Camassia, Colchicum, Crinum, Crocus, Cyclamen, Cyrtanthus, Dahlia, Dierama, Eucharis, Leucojum, Lycoris, Nerine, Scadoxus, Schizostylis, Sternbergia, Tritonia, Watsonia, Zephyranthes.

Order: place order for spring-flowering bulbs. Check the pages of gardening magazines for mail-order suppliers. When buying bulbs in bulk from garden centres, look for firm, weighty specimens without soft spots, bruises or damage. Flaking outer coverings are normal.

Plant: in cold climates, plant spring-flowering bulbs into prepared sites. Wait another month or two in warm areas.

Pot: spring bulbs for forcing should be potted up now. In warm climates, pot into refrigerated potting mix and then refrigerate potted bulbs for the next 12 weeks. In cold climates, place pots outside, covered to exclude light, for their chilling period.

Restart: summer-dormant bulbs grown and stored in their containers can be brought out and restarted into growth by saturating the soil. It will be necessary to mix a wetting agent into the water.

In greenhouses: empty and clean greenhouses. Inspect pots and benches for signs of insects or diseases and fumigate if necessary. Remove any whitewash or shadecloth that was applied before summer.

Hippeastrums: in cold climates, potted Hippeastrums can be started into growth for winter bloom. Give them 13°C (55°F) at night; 21°C (70°F) during the day. Keep lightly moist until flower buds appear, then water more generously.

Pest watch: slugs and snails are active again and can quickly destroy succulent new growth. Bait or spray.

Mid-autumn

In bloom: Camassia, Colchicum, Crinum, Crocus, Cyclamen, Dahlia, Leucojum, Nerine, Schizostylis, Zephyranthes.

Plant: continue to plant spring-flowering bulbs. Remember that cool soil – under 11°C (52°F) – is essential for cold-climate bulbs.

Mulch: in cold climates, apply a thick mulch over the top of spring-flowering bulbs. This helps to stabilise soil temperature and prevents repeated freezing and thawing of the soil. Mulch is also beneficial in frost-free areas; it improves soil texture.

Water: water newly planted spring bulbs. They make their roots during autumn and winter and some soil moisture is essential.

If the weather remains dry, give enough water to keep bulbs just moist.

Lift: in cool and cold climates, lift summer bulbs that have died back. Clean bulbs, check for damage or disease; discard those affected and store others in a dark, airy place that remains above freezing. Dust with, or dip bulbs into insecticide and fungicide. Do not store in plastic or other airtight containers. In warmer climates, the lifting of summer bulbs can be delayed until mid-winter.

Label: label colour varieties of lifted bulbs for easy identification when replanting.

Late autumn

In bloom: Camassia, Crinum, Crocus, Cyclamen, Eucharis, Moraea, Narcissus, Nerine, Oxalis, Polyxena, Schizostylis, Veltheimia.

Plant: in warm climates, plant lilies in deeply dug, improved soil.

Water: keep winter-growing bulbs moist from the time growth appears. They are from areas that receive most of their rain from now until early spring.

In greenhouses: in cold climates, tender, winter-growing bulbs will need night temperatures above freezing while those from the tropics will need a night-time minimum of at least 10°C (50°F), or possibly 15°C (59°F).

WINTER

June, July, August (southern hemisphere)
December, January, February (northern hemisphere)

Early winter

In bloom: Crocus, Cyclamen, Eucharis, Hippeastrum (forced), Moraea, Oxalis, Polyxena, Veltheimia.

Plant: in warm climates, spring bulbs which require cool soil – such as tulips and hyacinths – can be planted now.

Water: in warm climates, continue to water winter-growing bulbs if the weather is dry.

Inspect: check stored summer bulbs for signs of rot, insect attack or shrivelling. Fumigate if necessary. If bulbs are shrivelling, transfer them to a container of just moist sphagnum or peat moss; you should not be able to squeeze any water from the medium.

Cyclamen: potted Cyclamen will be in full bloom now. As the flowers fade, remove them by twisting and pulling the stems. Cyclamen will last longer if they are given cool conditions overnight. In mild climates, place outside overnight; in cold climates, move to an airy, unheated room overnight.

Forced bulbs: spring bulbs potted for forcing can be brought out from their place of chilling. Stand the pot in a cool, bright, but not sunny spot until the shoots turn green. Bring pot indoors when flower buds appear. Keep away from heaters and electrical appliances.

Mid-winter

In bloom: Crocus, Cyclamen, Geissorhiza, Ipheion, Lachenalia, Moraea, Oxalis, Spiloxene, Veltheimia.

Lift: in warm climates, winter-dormant bulbs that need separation and replanting can be lifted now. Retain only the biggest and healthiest-looking for replanting. Discard any damaged or diseased stock. Lifted bulbs can be either replanted immediately into refurbished soil or stored until spring.

Water: Winter-growing bulbs, whether in the garden or potted in greenhouses, must be kept watered. Many of them will be forming their flowers now.

Late winter

In bloom: Anemone, Babiana, Baeometra, Chionodoxa, Crocus, Cyclamen, Eranthis, Ferraria, Freesia, Galanthus, Geissorhiza, Hyacinthoides, Hyacinthus, Ipheion, Ixia, Lachenalia, Leopoldia, Muscari, Ornithogalum, Oxalis, Ranunculus, Scadoxus, Spiloxene, Tecophilaea, Tritonia, Tulipa, Veltheimia, Wurmbea.

Prepare: in warm climates, dig over and improve sites for new plantings of summer bulbs. Add complete plant food and compost or rotted manure, water in and let lie. In cooler climates, do this when the ground has thawed.

Deadhead: remove dead flowers from winter-growing bulbs, unless seeds are wanted, as the flowers will fade now.

Mulch: in cold climates, where thick layers of mulch have been used to protect bulbs from frost, scrape the mulch back to about 8cm (3in) in depth. Bulbs, especially small bulbs, will not grow through very thick layers of mulch. It is best to attempt this when night temperatures are consistently warmer than -5°C (23°F).

Order: summer-growing bulbs can be ordered now. If the soil is not frozen or too wet, you can also prepare the planting site for them. Dig in some rotted organic matter and a ration of complete plant food.

Start: In cold climates, summer-growing bulbs, such as Achimenes, Begonia, Gloriosa and Sandersonia, can be given an early start in pots indoors now. Keep them warm – about 16°C (61°F) – and give bright light as soon as shoots are seen.

Bulbs to Plant in
Late Summer/Autumn

Bulbs in this section are planted towards the end of summer or in autumn. Some may be planted at other times,

depending on your climate. If so, this is noted in the "Planting tips" section of individual entries.

All plant dimensions and planting depths are given in metric and imperial measurements. The conversions have been rounded off to the nearest whole number.

Allium

Ornamental onion

Family: *Alliaceae (the onion family, previously Liliaceae).*
Type: *bulb.* **Native to:** *different species native to Europe, Asia Minor, Central Asia, East Asia and western North America where the winters are cool to cold. The rainfall varies over this wide area.*

■ **Preferred climate:** a wide range of cold, cool and mild climates as the many species come from diverse parts of the northern hemisphere. They are least suited to subtropical and tropical gardens.

■ **Planting tips:** plant in autumn 10-13cm (4-5in) deep in well-drained, sandy soil with a pH of 6-7. Full sun or part shade suits.

■ **Growing season:** during spring and summer. Eventual height depends on the species; the tallest reaches more than 1m (3ft).

■ **Flowering season:** spring or summer, depending on the species in white, yellow, mauve, rosy-pink or red. One species, *Allium subhirsutum*, is sweetly scented.

■ **Care:** keep moist after growth begins. Little or no fertiliser is needed if the soil is good. Allow to dry when foliage begins to yellow.

■ **In pots:** *A. neapolitanum* and *A. karataviense* are the most suitable species for containers. Pot in autumn and keep at about 7°C (45°F) until roots have formed.

Below left: Spectacular Allium giganteum *is one of the biggest species. Its ornate flower heads, over 1m (3ft) tall, look great in fresh or dried arrangements.*

Below, centre: The golden garlic, A. moly, flowers mid-summer on 30cm (12in) stems. A bright plant, it is inclined to spread.

Below: A. carinatum subsp. pulchellum, from southern Europe, grows to 60cm (2ft). Exotic flowers appear in mid to late summer.

Joy Harland / Photos Horticultural / Lorna Rose

Anomatheca

(Syn. Lapeirousia), Flame Freesia

Family: *Iridaceae (Iris family).*
Type: *corm.* **Native to:** *northern and eastern South Africa where the winters are warm and fairly dry.*

■ **Preferred climate:** subtropical, frost-free and near frost-free areas. Accepts -5°C (23°F) with little or no damage to foliage if it is sheltered by overhanging evergreen foliage. Grows in milder parts of the UK.

■ **Planting tips:** plant in early autumn or, in cold climates, spring, 8-10cm (3-4in) deep in well-drained, sandy soil that contains organic matter. A soil pH of 5.5-7 is ideal. Plants accept full sun, part-shade or dappled shade; sun is best in cooler areas.

■ **Growing season:** in mild climates in autumn, winter and spring to a height of 30-45cm (12-18in). In cooler places, such as the UK, the plant remains dormant in winter and may only reach a height of 15-17cm (6-7in).

■ **Flowering season:** for a long period early to mid-spring in its homeland and similar climates; encroaching on summer in cooler climates. Flowers are rosy red with darker central blotches on their lower petals.

■ **Care:** little needed as plants can look after themselves if rainfall is regular during the growing season. In very cold places, lift bulbs when they die back and store above freezing until spring.

■ **In pots:** possible but not well suited to pot culture.

Right, top: From sky blue to almost violet, Camassia comes in a range of eye-catching flower colours.

Right, bottom: Bright and beautiful flame Freesia, Lapeirousia grandiflora, ***flowers for a long time from early spring.***

Jerry Harpur / Jack Hobbs / Photos Horticultural

Camassia

Camass, Quamash, Camosh, Wild hyacinth

Family: *Liliaceae (Lily family).*
Type: *bulb.* **Native to:** *western North America, mid-western and southern USA and western South America where the climate varies from generally wet but driest in summer, to generally dry with rainfall evenly spread, to generally wet with the warmer months being the wettest.*

■ **Preferred climate:** cold, cool and mild areas where soils are moist, deep and fertile. Worth trying in frost-free gardens. Bulbs are hardy to -29°C (-20°F) but, where such temperatures are not accompanied by a blanket of snow, a thick layer of mulch is essential. Not a good choice for dry soils.

■ **Planting tips:** in early autumn, 10cm (4in) deep, the same distance apart, in fairly rich, fertile soil. If sandy, it should contain a lot of moisture-retentive organic matter. While plants cannot accept constant bogginess, they enjoy the well-drained edges of boggy places where they have easy access to water. Full sun or part shade suits, the latter if there is a risk of drying out. The best effect is achieved with a massed planting.

■ **Growing season:** spring, summer and early autumn to 30-90cm (1-3ft) tall, depending on the species.

■ **Flowering season:** mid to late spring or early summer, except the South American species, *Camassia biflora*, which blooms in autumn.

■ **Care:** ensure that the soil stays moist when plants are in leaf. Lift and divide bulbs only when necessary. If winters are long and frigid, mulch after the bulbs become dormant.

■ **In pots:** not usually grown in pots as a few bulbs do not produce a remarkable effect.

Chionodoxa

Glory of the snow

Family: *Liliaceae (Lily family).*
Type: *bulb.* **Native to:** *mountains of Cyprus, Crete and western Turkey where the climate is Mediterranean with severe winters and deep snow. Highland summers are mild to warm and relatively dry.*

■ **Preferred climate:** cool to cold areas with moisture in winter and spring. They need winter chilling to flower successfully. Can be grown in pots and refrigerated for mid-winter bloom in both warm and cold areas. When covered with snow, bulbs are hardy to -29°C (-20°F).

■ **Planting tips:** plant in early to mid-autumn 8-13cm (3-5in) deep, the same distance apart, in acidic, well-drained gravelly or gritty soil made moisture-retentive with rotted organic matter. Full sun is essential in winter and spring. Plants can be grown beneath late-leafing deciduous trees, in rockery pockets or dry stone walls. Site them where they can be left alone with little root competition.

■ **Growing season:** late winter to late spring to 15-20cm (6-8in) tall.

■ **Flowering season:** late winter, the white-centred blue flowers often appearing through remaining snow. Different species have flowers in pink, mauve, white or various shades of blue.

■ **Care:** must have moisture in winter for root development and through spring until leaves wither. Where snow always falls in winter, melt-water is adequate. In snowless cold climates, ensure that the soil is moisture-retentive and mulch bulbs heavily in autumn. Scrape away most mulch in late winter. No feeding is necessary if soil is humus-rich.

■ **In pots:** add sand or fine gravel to potting mix to ensure good drainage and plant bulbs fairly close together – about ten in a 15cm (6in) pot. For mid-winter blooms, pot in autumn and chill below 7°C (45°F) but above 0°C (32°F) for 8 weeks. Bring into cool temperatures – not above 12°C (54°F) – until shoots appear, then place in their flowering position.

*Above: Glory of the snow, Chionodoxa luciliae, **is one of the earliest spring flowers, often appearing through snow. It is for colder climates only.***

Colchicum

Autumn Crocus, Naked boys, Naked ladies, Meadow saffron

Family: *Liliaceae (Lily family). There are two categories, autumn-flowering and winter/spring-flowering.* **Type:** *corm.* **Native to:** *UK, Europe, North Africa, Middle East, Asia Minor, Central Asia, northern India, south-western China where the climate varies over this huge area from cool Mediterranean to rainy or snowy year-round. Winters are always cool, often cold to very cold.*

■ **Preferred climate:** basically cool and cold climates, although these plants are more tolerant of frost-free conditions than might be expected. The autumn-flowering types, especially, do not require winter chilling and are worth trying in the cooler frost-free climates. The hardiest species are those from Europe, the mountains of Turkey, Iran and the Caucasus. They will tolerate -29°C (-20°F). The least

hardy, from coastal parts of Turkey and Greece, tolerate -7°C (19°F). The most popular of the grown species flower in autumn, the winter and spring-flowering types being less common in gardens except for the yellow-flowered *Colchicum luteum*.

■ **Planting tips:** plant mid to late summer in well-drained, sandy, moisture-retentive soil, 10-13cm (4-5in) below the surface. Plants accept full sun, dappled shade or part-shade.

■ **Growing season:** autumn-flowering types grow during late winter and spring. Winter/spring flowering species grow in spring and early summer. Sizes vary but 20cm (8in) is about the maximum height. The strappy leaves can be widespreading.

■ **Flowering season:** autumn or winter/spring. While most species flower in shades of rosy or mauve-pink, there are white varieties. Afghanistan's *C. luteum* is the only yellow-flowered species.

■ **Care:** ensure adequate water while plants are in leaf, then allow to dry out. Don't disturb established clumps frequently. Lift and separate at the end of the foliage season, then replant immediately.

■ **In pots:** not very good pot plants as outer flowers fall over soon after opening and leaves are big and untidy. Corms will flower without any soil or water if placed in a bright room.

Below, left: Colchicum speciosum is perhaps the brightest of the autumn-flowering types and comes in several colours.

Below: Colchicums have been widely hybridised. This is the double-flowered form, 'Water lily'.

Right: Colchicums produce their elegant, goblet-shaped flowers well before the leaves.

Jack Hobbs/Jerry Harpur;Beth Chatto's garden;Auscape

Jerry Harpur/Cadogan Place/Auscape/Gabe Palmer/Stock Photos/Michael Viard/Auscape

Crocus

Family: *Iridaceae (Iris family). Two categories; autumn-flowering and winter/spring-flowering.* **Type:** *corm.* **Native to:** *central and southern Europe, the Middle East, North Africa, Asia Minor, Central Asia and western China. Many species are from Mediterranean climates with winters that range from cool to severe but always wet, followed by hot, dry summers. Other species are from high altitude meadows that are snowbound in winter and moist from melt-water and rain in spring and summer. One common factor is low temperatures in winter – even the mildest habitat is at least frosty. Many species are hardy to -35˚C (-31˚F).*

■ **Preferred climate:** best in cold and cool climates. If summers are fairly dry, the autumn-flowering species are more successful in frost-free gardens than winter or spring-flowering species. But Crocuses are generally not good choices for frost-free, lowland gardens. If pre-cooled and grown in chilled potting mix, bulbs may be raised in pots in warm areas.

■ **Planting tips:** plant autumn-flowering species in late summer; winter/spring-flowering species in early autumn. Plant corms 5-8cm (2-3in) deep – deeper in warm areas – and about the same distance apart in very well-drained, moderately acidic soil enriched with rotted organic matter. Bulbs do best in full sun. They can be planted under grass but only in cold areas where grass growth slows in autumn and ceases in winter.

■ **Growing season:** leaves of the autumn-flowering species appear just before, with or after the flowers. Winter/spring-flowering species grow through the spring and summer. The total height of the plants is usually under 20cm (8in).

■ **Flowering season:** in white and shades of mauve, pink and yellow, appearing in autumn, winter, spring and early summer, depending on the species.

■ **Care:** keep moist when plants are in leaf. Clumps may be fed with complete plant food or slow-release fertiliser when growth begins. Never cut the leaves while they are still green.

■ **In pots:** Crocus is one of the best bulbs for pots but they must be chilled below 7˚C (45˚F) for 8 weeks after they are potted; then bring into a cool place, about 12˚C (54˚F), until shoots appear. Bring into a bright room to flower.

Left: Crocuses are ideal for naturalising under deciduous trees. Here, they glow in the early spring sun before the tree canopy develops.

Above, left: Stark and stunning, Crocus not only tolerate the extreme cold, they need it to bloom.

Above: There are many Crocus hybrids with bigger, beautifully coloured or patterned flowers. This is the popular hybrid, 'Pickwick'.

Cyclamen

Persian violet, Alpine violet, Sowbread

Family: *Primulaceae (Primrose family).* **Type:** *tuber.* **Native to:** *southern Europe, North Africa, Turkey, Caucasus, Iran where the climate is predominantly Mediterranean with winters ranging from cool along the coast to severe in highland parts. Some species are from alpine meadows where rain in summer is expected.*

■ **Preferred climate:** frost-free, cool and cold climates, preferably with a Mediterranean climate. Plants can tolerate some summer rain if the soil drains freely. Generally, Cyclamen can tolerate winter lows of -18˚C (0˚F). Species from Mediterranean islands or coastal climates, e.g., *Cyclamen graecum, C. africanum* and *C. persicum,* are almost intolerant of frosts, while those from alpine areas are most cold-resistant.

■ **Planting tips:** plant in autumn, just beneath the surface of well-drained humus-enriched soil which may be acidic, neutral or slightly alkaline. The big-flowered florists' Cyclamen prefers its tuber to break the surface. The best position for Cyclamen is among trees and open shrubs which provide shelter and shade and soak up excess water which would otherwise rot the tubers.

■ **Growing season:** autumn, winter and spring, except evergreen *C. purpurascens* which also grows through summer. Plants vary in height and spread, although none can be described as big.

■ **Flowering season:** autumn, winter or early spring in white or shades of pink, mauve, purple or red.

■ **Care:** apply a thin mulch of compost or leaf mould in late spring. Feed sparingly with complete plant food when new growth begins. Cyclamen will generally live on rain but, if the cooler months are unusually dry, water will be needed. Do not disturb unnecessarily.

■ **In pots:** plant with top of the tuber at surface of porous potting mix. Keep moist and feed lightly but often during growth. Start to dry out as summer nears. Tubers may be stored dry over summer in their pots.

Eranthis

Winter aconite

Family: *Ranunculaceae (Ranunculus family).* **Type:** *tuber.* **Native to:** *southern Europe, Balkans, Asia Minor, Central Asia, East Asia and Japan where the climate varies but winters are always cool to cold; summers may be dry or rainy.*

■ **Preferred climate:** cool and cold-winter climates. Plants need to experience temperatures below -6˚C (20˚F) to succeed. They are hardy to about -34˚C (-30˚F).

■ **Planting tips:** Plant fresh tubers in summer or early autumn. If tubers look shrivelled, soak them overnight in warm water, then plant 8cm (3in) deep, the same distance apart, in fertile, humus-rich soil that drains freely yet retains moisture. Plants do best in soils with a pH of 6-8. Winter sun is essential but, as Eranthis are native to deciduous woodlands, shade is necessary in late spring and summer. If grown under evergreen trees or shrubs, plant on the sunny side. Eranthis look best planted in big drifts.

■ **Growing season:** Winter, spring and early summer to about 10cm (4in) with a lesser spread.

■ **Flowering season:** late winter or very early spring, often appearing through snow. Flowers are bright yellow or, in the case of *Eranthis pinnatifida*, white.

■ **Care:** needs consistent moisture through winter and spring. They accept summer dryness but will tolerate watering if soil drains well. No feeding is necessary if soil is humus-rich from falling leaves. Propagate by seeds scattered onto loosened soil. Eranthis don't like to be disturbed. If essential, divide straight after blooming and replant divisions at once.

■ **In pots:** plant shallowly, about 5cm (2in) apart, and just cover with humus-rich potting mix rather than sandy potting mix. Water and place in a cool, shady spot to establish. Bring into the sun in late autumn, then indoors when flower buds appear. After blooming, plant in the garden. Next year, pot new tubers.

Erythronium

Dog tooth violet, Trout lily, Fawn lily, Avalanche lily, Adder's tongue, Lamb's tongue

Family: *Liliaceae (Lily family).*
Type: *corm.* **Native to:** *mostly the north-western States of the USA and western Canada, a few in the east of those countries. One species,* **Erythronium dens-canis**, *is from Europe. Their native climates are cool to cold with snowy or rainy winters, followed by warm or hot summers with rain.*

■ **Preferred climate:** cool and cold-climate gardens but they are worth trying in frost-free areas. Some species are hardy to -40°C (-40°F) and all are hardy to at least -15°C (5°F).

■ **Planting tips:** late summer or early autumn 8cm (3in) deep and 10cm (4in) apart. All species demand

good drainage but are not fussy about their soil. The best results are achieved in friable soil that contains a lot of rotted organic matter. Plants accept winter sun in cold and cool climates but like the protection of dappled shade in spring and summer where those seasons are hot.

■ **Growing season:** late winter and spring. The height and spread of plants varies depending on the species, but typically they are about 30cm (12in) tall with a lesser spread.

■ **Flowering season:** early, mid or late spring, depending on the species and your climate; the cooler the climate, the later the flowers appear. Flowers may be white, cream, pink or purple.

■ **Care:** ensure that corms are well watered from the time growth appears until summer. Mulch lightly in autumn with compost or leaf mould. When clumps become overcrowded, lift and divide in summer or early autumn, then replant immediately in refurbished soil. Disturb plants as infrequently as possible.

■ **In pots:** not usually raised in pots; better in drifts in the garden.

Far left: Cyclamen hederifolium and dog tooth violet, Erythronium, make a vibrant ground covering duo beneath deciduous trees and shrubs.

Left: Eranthis x tubergenii is a hybrid with bigger flowers than the usual species. Mass plant it for the best effect.

Above: Erythronium 'Pagoda' produces plenty of big, cream-yellow flowers on large-sized plants.

Ferraria

Starfish flower

Family: *Iridaceae (Iris family).*
Type: *corm.* **Native to:** *mostly the coast and near inland of western and north-western South Africa and Namibia where there is a Mediterranean climate with low annual rainfall concentrated mostly in the cooler months.*

■ **Preferred climate:** frost-free and near frost-free climates, including the coast. Plants will accept overnight lows of -6˚C (21˚F) but expect winter days to be in the 10-20˚C (50-68˚F) range. Summer rain is tolerated if plants are grown in deep, sandy soil. In colder areas where spring is rainy and summers mild, try planting in early spring when frosts have almost finished.

■ **Planting tips:** plant in autumn 10cm (4in) deep, 15cm (6in) apart, in sandy, gravelly soil with some rotted manure added. Full sun is essential.

■ **Growing season:** in autumn, winter and spring in mild areas, in late winter, spring and early summer in cooler climates. Plants grow to about 50cm (20in), sometimes more.

■ **Flowering season:** late winter to mid-spring (late spring in colder areas).

■ **Care:** needs consistent watering during autumn, winter and spring but can tolerate dryness in summer. In good soil no feeding is necessary, but in coastal, sandy soil apply a ration of complete plant food when growth appears.

■ **In pots:** not very suitable for pots as they like deep soil.

Freesia

Family: *Iridaceae (Iris family).*
Type: *corm.* **Native to:** *southern and south-western South Africa where the climate is warm with little or no frost. In part of the area, rainfall is concentrated during the cooler months, elsewhere it is more evenly distributed.*

■ **Preferred climate:** frost-free, near frost-free and subtropical climates. In colder but not very cold places, they can be planted in spring for summer blooms. In growth, Freesias cannot tolerate sharp or frequent frosts. When bulbs are dormant in summer, they will tolerate heavy rain if drainage is adequate.

■ **Planting tips:** in autumn in mild climates, early spring where winters are sharply frosty or snowy. Plant 5cm (2in) deep, 8cm (3in) apart, in any well-drained, friable, fertile soil.

■ **Growing season:** autumn, winter and spring, or spring and summer, depending on when they

are planted, to about 30cm (12in) tall. Plants do not usually remain erect but fall about somewhat untidily.

■ **Flowering season:** late winter/spring or summer – sometimes with a repeat in autumn. Flowers are white, cream, yellow, pink, mauve, red or orange. Natural species are richly and sweetly fragrant, hybrids less so. All are terrific as cut flowers.

■ **Care:** keep moist during the growing season and lightly dig in a ration of slow-release fertiliser when growth begins. Alternatively, feed monthly with liquid organic plant food. Don't water or feed after blooming. In cold climates, lift bulbs after first frost and store above freezing until spring.

■ **In pots:** grow in tall, rather than squat pots, and place corms about 3cm (1in) apart. Keep moist and feed monthly with liquid organic fertiliser. If possible, grow outside in the sun, otherwise in a heated greenhouse or very bright, sunny room.

Left, top: The stunning flowers of Ferraria crispa *are unusually coloured and ruffled. They appear in succession.*

Left, bottom: The curious starfish flower is sturdy enough to resist coastal winds and summer droughts.

Above, left: Colourful and easy to grow, Freesias have one of the sweetest fragrances of any flower.

Above, right: Freesia hybrids come in attractive new colours, such as this pretty dark red and yellow combination.

Lorna Rose/Jerry Harpur;Beth Chatto's Garden/Photos Horticultural

Left: The crown imperial, *Fritillaria imperialis,* **is the most striking and desirable of all fritillaries but can be hard to grow.**

Inset, left: The spring flowers of *F. raddeana* **look stylish but smell like skunk.**

Inset, right: *F. michailovskyi* **from Turkey reaches 20cm (8in) and flowers in early summer.**

Fritillaria

Fritillary

Family: *Liliaceae (Lily family).*
Type: *bulb.* **Native to:** *European countries around the Mediterranean, Asia Minor, central Asia, east Asia, Japan and the western US and Canada from sea level to the snow line. Winters are at least cool, in some places very cold; summers may be hot and fairly dry or rainy.*

■ **Preferred climate:** cool and cold climates. The most popular species are quite hardy and able to tolerate many degrees of frost, some lesser known species do not expect winters to be sharply frosty. No fritillary is suited to warm, humid, frost-free areas.

■ **Planting tips:** plant in late summer or early autumn 8cm (3in) deep, 15cm (6in) apart, except for the crown imperial which needs a depth of 20cm (8in) and spacing of 35cm (14in). A clay loam, high in organic matter and with a neutral pH, is best, although any good well-drained soil will do. Full sun in winter and spring is essential.

■ **Growing season:** winter, spring and early summer. Most species are relatively low-growing but the crown imperial can have flower stems 1m (3ft) tall.

■ **Flowering season:** spring. Apart from the crown imperial which has striking orange or yellow flowers, most fritillaries have subtly coloured, small blooms. Nevertheless, they are charming and some are curiously patterned.

■ **Care:** keep moist during winter and spring and feed with complete plant food at the first sign of growth. After blooming, water can be withheld. When plants die down, mulch with rotted manure or compost.

■ **In pots:** the smaller fritillaries make delightful pot plants. It is possible to grow crown imperials in containers, but their size dictates very large tubs.

Galanthus

Snowdrop

Family: *Amaryllidaceae (Hippeastrum family).* **Type:** *bulb.*
Native to: *woodlands of Europe, Asia Minor, Russia and Iran where the winters are wet and/or snowy and always cool, often very cold. The summers are warm with rain or hot and dry.*

■ **Preferred climate:** cool and cold climates. The bulbs will not do well where winter overnight lows are much above freezing. They can tolerate temperatures down to -34˚C (-30˚F) and are happiest where winter nights are below freezing and the days rarely warmer than 7˚C (45˚F).

■ **Planting tips:** plant as soon as bulbs become available in early autumn. Once out of the ground, the bulbs dry fast. If this occurs, growth and flowering will be poor. Buy only freshly dug stock. Plant 8cm (3in) deep, the same distance apart, in humus-rich, well-drained clay loam with a neutral or just alkaline pH (pH 7-8). In very cold climates, plants will accept sun but the light shade of deciduous branches and stems is a more natural setting. Galanthus can be grown under high-branched evergreen trees.

■ **Growing season:** autumn, winter and early spring, depending on the species. All are small, rarely exceeding 20cm (8in) in height.

■ **Flowering season:** late winter or early spring. The white flowers often appear through snow.

■ **Care:** keep evenly moist always and mulch with compost or rotted manure when leaves die down. Disturb as infrequently as possible. If necessary, lift, separate and replant immediately after blooming while the leaves are still green.

■ **In pots:** plant 3cm (1in) deep, the same distance apart. Grow in unheated greenhouse or outside in cool conditions. Bring indoors when buds develop but keep away from bright sunshine, heaters or very warm rooms.

Above: A delightful small bulb, snowdrops,** Galanthus nivalis, **must endure a cold winter to succeed.

Galtonia

Cape hyacinth, Summer hyacinth, Berg lily

Family: *Liliaceae (Lily family).*
Type: *bulb.* **Native to:** *eastern South Africa where the winters are cool, with extreme lows of -7°C (19°F), or frost-free, depending on the altitude. Rain falls throughout the year but winters are much drier than summers.*

■ **Preferred climate:** tropical, subtropical, frost-free and, possibly, cool climate gardens. If a thick covering of mulch is laid over the bulbs after the top growth has died back in autumn, Galtonias can tolerate temperatures down to at least -15°C (5°F), possibly much lower for short periods. Bulbs should not be lifted every year.

■ **Planting tips:** plant in autumn or early spring in mild climates, early spring in colder places. Plant shallowly, just below the surface but about 45cm (18in) apart in deep, friable, well-drained soil in full sun.

Choose a spot where these big plants can be left alone for several years.

■ **Growing season:** spring, summer and early autumn to 1m (3ft) and more in height. The thick leaves form a rosette at the base of the plant.

■ **Flowering season:** early to mid-summer. Popular *Galtonia candicans* has white flowers, while the two other species sometimes offered have pale green blooms.

■ **Care:** keep well watered during the growing season and apply a ration of complete plant food at the first sign of growth. After plants die down in autumn, a mulch of rotted manure will help to keep plants vigorous. Slugs and snails are attracted to the leaves and can make clumps look very untidy by the end of summer. Increase your stock by sowing seed in spring rather than by separating offsets.

■ **In pots:** possible, but the size of the plant dictates very large tubs.

Geissorhiza

Wine cups, Sequins

Family: *Iridaceae (Iris family).*
Type: *corm.* **Native to:** *western Namibia, western and south-western South Africa where the climate is fairly dry with most rain falling from mid-autumn to early spring. Winters are frost-free or near frost-free; summers dry to very dry and hot.*

■ **Preferred climate:** subtropical, frost-free and near frost-free climates. In their native ranges, frosts are possible but not common and days are almost always above 10°C (50°F). In cold climates, grow in pots in cool greenhouses.

■ **Planting tips:** plant in autumn 3-5cm (1-2in) deep and apart in average soil of resonable fertility. Plants need full sun or a few hours' light midday shade.

■ **Growing season:** autumn, winter and early spring usually to a height of less than 15cm (6in). Its leaves are sparse and narrow.

Jack Hobbs

■ **Flowering season:** mid to late winter. The flowers are striking, some breathtaking, and come in a variety of colours, including some beautiful blues. Bi- and tri-coloured flowers are also produced.

■ **Care:** give plenty of water from the time growth begins. Gradually reduce watering after flowers fade, letting plants dry out during the last month of summer. If soil drains well, moderate summer rain or watering will not harm the corms. Geissorhiza do not need feeding if the soil is good; if not, two or three thin layers of rotted organic matter, applied at intervals after growth dies back, is beneficial. In the monsoonal tropics, lift bulbs before the onset of the wet season or grow in pots kept undercover.

■ **In pots:** all species grow well in pots and, as they are small, rather delicate-looking plants, this can be the best way to raise them. After flowers fade, keep pots just moist.

*Left: Galtonia princeps **is a fairly rare small species with pale green flowers in late winter.***

***Right, top: Geissorhiza is a big genus of many varied, lovely bulbs. This is** G. inflexa.*

Right, bottom:** G. tulbaghensis **has white flowers with striking, dark centres.

Gladiolus

Family: *Iridaceae (Iris family).*
Type: *corm.* **Native to:** *mostly southern Africa but also North Africa, the Middle East and Mediterranean Europe. The climate there varies but most species come from Mediterranean climates, i.e. wet winters that are cool or mild, followed by warm to hot, dry summers. Some of the southern African species come from places with year-round or summer dominant rain. Winters there are nearly frost-free.*

■ **Preferred climate:** any with a growing season of at least 110 days. In frost-free and near frost-free areas, Gladiolus can be grown year-round as both summer and winter-growing species are available.

■ **Planting tips:** plant in early autumn for winter-growing types; spring for summer growers, 13cm (5in) deep, 17cm (7in) apart. Well-drained, sandy soil containing plenty of compost is best but Gladiolus will grow in any well-drained, fertile soil that is a little on the acidic side. Use animal manures sparingly or not at all as these have been linked with rotting in Gladiolus. A site in full sun produces the best floral display.

■ **Growing season:** autumn, winter and spring to 1.5m (5ft) tall, depending on the species or hybrid.

■ **Flowering season:** autumn-planted, winter-growing species flower in spring. Spring-planted, spring and summer-growing species flower in summer or autumn. Plants generally flower about 100 days after planting so, in places with long growing seasons, staggered plantings can produce very long displays. In frost-free and near frost-free gardens, it's possible to grow both the winter and summer-growing species and have Gladiolus flowers for much of the year. A big range of colours is available, some with lovely patterns.

■ **Care:** keep evenly moist from the time growth begins until leaves start to wither. Where frosts are not severe, corms can be left in the ground. Elsewhere, lift corms after leaves wither in autumn, clean and store above-freezing in an airy, dark place until replanting time in spring. Check lifted bulbs for signs of softness, rot, mould or insect invasion; discard any that are suspect. If mould is a problem, bulbs can be dusted with fungicide powder or dipped in a fungicide solution before storing.

■ **In pots:** taller species are not usually grown in pots as they can easily become top-heavy. Smaller Gladiolus make wonderful container plants and, as many species can be rather invasive in mild climates, pots are a good way to prevent future problems.

Left: From the Mediterranean region, hardy Gladiolus communis subsp. *byzantinus,* **starts to grow in early spring, and produces flowers in early summer.**

Inset, from left: All from South Africa, G. cardinalis *is a hardy, winter-growing species;* G. carinatus *is strongly scented;* G. alatus *flowers in early spring and grows to 30cm (12in).*

Above: G. tristis *is from the winter rainfall Cape region of South Africa. It grows through the winter, producing its big, nocturnally fragrant flowers in early spring.*

Hyacinthoides

(Syn. Endymion, Scilla), Bluebell

Family: *Liliaceae (Lily family).*
Type: *bulb.* **Native to:** *western Europe, south-western Europe, Italy and North Africa where the winters are cold, cool or frost-free, depending on the latitude and elevation. Summers are cool to hot.*

■ **Preferred climate:** cold, cool and frost-free gardens. Plants are hardy to -34˚C (-30˚F) but are also happy to grow in frost-free gardens out of the tropics.

■ **Planting tips:** plant in autumn 10cm (4in) deep and apart in well-drained, humus-rich soil that's a little on the heavy side. Blubells are plants of the deciduous forests where they receive a mulch of fallen leaves each year. They are best planted in broad drifts beneath deciduous trees, rather than in small clumps in more developed parts of the garden, because their leaves are too floppy and untidy for close-up view. Plants prefer part-shade and the flowers look and last better when they are not exposed to full sun.

■ **Growing season:** winter and spring up to 50cm (20in) tall. Leaves are long and strappy and, while erect at first, they soon fall on the ground around the flowers.

■ **Flowering season:** early to mid-spring in blue, white or pink.

■ **Care:** irrigate if rain is irregular during autumn and winter. No feeding is necessary in fertile soil that is mulched annually.

■ **In pots:** not grown in pots as the flowering season is short and the leaves are untidy.

*Above, left: Habranthus robustus **is a plant-and-forget bulb for warm-climate gardens.***

Right: Hide their coarse foliage by placing bluebells among other spring flowers such as these forget-me-nots.

Habranthus

Family: *Amaryllidaceae (Hippeastrum family).* **Type:** *bulb.*
Native to: *north Argentina, Uruguay, Paraguay and south Brazil. The climate there is humid and subtropical. Rain falls in every month and there are no distinct wet or dry seasons. Winters are frost-free or near frost-free. While lows of -10˚C (14˚F) are possible in inland or highland parts, they do not occur often.*

■ **Preferred climate:** tropical, subtropical, frost-free and near frost-free gardens. Possible in pots in greenhouses kept above freezing at night and about 15˚C (59˚F) during the day.

■ **Planting tips:** plant in early autumn 5cm (2in) deep and 5-10cm (2-4in) apart. Soil must drain freely and be reasonably fertile. Full sun is the best aspect, although the plants will accept a few hours' shade each day. Good beneath low ground covers. In frost-free climates, Habranthus multiply fast, both by seed and from offsets. Plant first where they can be contained to test the reaction to your garden.

■ **Growing season:** autumn, winter and early spring to 30cm (12in) or less, depending on the species.

■ **Flowering season:** summer, after the leaves have died back. They come in various shades of pink.

■ **Care:** ensure they receive adequate water during the growing season but allow them to dry out when the leaves begin to fade. Heavy summer showers often produce sudden flushes of flowers. Apply a ration of complete plant food once, at the beginning of the leaf-growing season. Remove flowers as they fade to prevent unwanted spread by seed.

■ **In pots:** all species give a lovely display in pots, especially in wide, shallow dishes. Plant the bulbs closely together, not touching, with their pointy ends at soil level. Keep moist from the time leaves appear and feed fortnightly with liquid organic fertiliser. Alloy to dry out when leaves start to wither. A thorough soaking a few weeks after the first flush of flowers will induce another flush of flowers.

Hyacinthus

Hyacinth

Family: *Liliaceae (Lily family).*
Type: *bulb.* **Native to***: soutnern Turkey, western Syria, Lebanon, and Iran where there is a Mediterranean climate. Most rain falls between mid-autumn and early spring; summers are hot and dry. In the higher parts of their range, Hyacinths are covered with snow.*

■ **Preferred climate:** cold, cool and near frost-free gardens. Bulbs are hardy to -34˚C (-30F). In other climates, hyacinths can be grown in containers and forced to bloom in winter. In warm climates this will require the refrigeration of the potted bulbs for 10-13 weeks – in colder climates, outside temperatures are usually low enough.

■ **Planting tips:** plant in autumn when soil temperatures have fallen to 11˚C (52˚F) or less. In cold climates, this may have occurred by the end of the first month of autumn. In near frost-free climates, it may not happen until the beginning of winter. Plant 8-13cm (3-5in) deep – deeper in near frost-free gardens – and 13-15cm (5-6in) apart in average, well-drained soil in sun.

■ **Growing season:** late winter and spring to about 25cm (10in) tall.

■ **Flowering season:** late winter or spring, depending on the climate – the warmer the climate, the earlier the flowers appear. Flowers may be white, cream, pink, red, lilac, blue or purple and are highly fragrant.

■ **Care:** keep moist while roots are forming in autumn and winter but allow to dry out when flowers finish. A light ration of complete plant food or slow-release granules at planting time is all the feeding hyacinths need. When leaves wither, lift, clean and store bulbs in a cool, dark airy place. Refrigerate two months before replanting in autumn. Flowers in second and subsequent years will not be as dense and spectacular as in the first year. If you want a dense display, discard the lifted bulbs and buy new stock for the following autumn.

■ **In pots:** beautiful potted plants for both the garden and home but note that a long, cool period – below 7˚C (44˚F) – is essential for good root formation. Without this, flowers may not appear at all. Read the section titled "Forcing Bulbs to Bloom" on page 26 for details.

Ipheion

Spring starflower

Family: *Alliaceae (Onion family).*
Type: *bulb.* **Native to:** *Uruguay and Argentina where the climate is mild to warm and rainy year-round. Extreme lows of -10˚C (14˚F) are possible inland.*

■ **Preferred climate:** frost-free, near frost-free and cool-climate gardens. In colder climates, grow in pots for a pretty tabletop display. In gardens, bulbs will accept -10˚C (14˚F) but, where such temperatures are common, the protection of a thick mulch laid in autumn is essential. Reduce this to a thin layer when frosts are almost finished.

■ **Planting tips:** plant in early autumn 5cm (2in) deep and 8cm (3in) apart in average, well-drained soil in a sunny spot.

■ **Growing season:** in frost-free climates, leaves appear about a week after planting and growth continues through autumn and winter, dying back in mid-summer. In colder climates, growth begins in early spring and continues through much of the summer.

■ **Flowering season:** mid-winter to early spring in frost-free climates, early to late spring in colder climates – the colder the climate, the later the flowers appear. Flowers are a lovely sky or deep blue; white ones are available as named hybrids. There is also a rare yellow species *Ipheion sellowianum.*

■ **Care:** keep moist from the time leaves appear until flowers fade. No feeding is necessary if soil is good. Ipheions tend to multiply fast, especially in frost-free climates.

■ **In pots:** in a wide, shallow dish, these bulbs put on a charming display for at least six weeks. Even the grey, grassy foliage is neat and attractive. Plant bulbs closely together, not touching, about 3cm (1in) below the surface in autumn. Water in immediately. Growth will appear within a week and, in frost-free gardens, first flowers will rise in the second month of winter. Prolong the blooming season by removing flower stems as they fade. After flowering, stop watering and leaves will soon begin to wither. When they have gone, store the pot in a dry, dark place until the following autumn. Every second year, unpot, separate the hundreds of bulbs and replant the biggest. In cold climates, pot in late winter and grow indoors until frosts have finished.

Left: A background of white Violas brings the violet hyacinths into sharp relief.

Above: 'Wisley Blue' is a deeper colour form of Ipheion uniflorum. There are other hybrids.

Lorna Rose / Brent Wilson / Jack Hobbs / Joy Harland

Left: Standing tall and majestic, Ixia viridiflora has flowers in an unusual soft green.

Inset: Ixia hybrids are available in a range of warm colours, including this red and gold.

Ixia

Corn lily, Wand flower

Family: *Iridaceae (Iris family).*
Type: *corm.* **Native to:**
south-western Cape Province of South Africa where the climate is Mediterranean. Most of the rain falls between mid-autumn and early spring.

■ **Preferred climate:** frost-free and near frost-free gardens, especially those with a Mediterranean climate. Plants can tolerate frosts of -5°C (25°F) but not often and not for long periods. In cold climates, grow in pots sheltered in a cool greenhouse where night temperatures are held above freezing.

■ **Planting tips:** plant in autumn 5-10cm (2-4in) deep, 15cm (6in) apart in deep, sandy or loamy soil in full sun.

■ **Growing season:** autumn, winter and spring, sometimes to well over 1m (3ft) tall but usually less. Plants multiply to form dense clumps of erect, grassy leaves.

■ **Flowering season:** late winter to early summer, depending on the species. Most species flower in the first half of spring. The flowers are pink, red, orange, yellow, white or a beautiful watery green.

■ **Care:** water the planting site in autumn, whether growth is visible

or not. Keep moist until flowering has finished, then allow to dry out. While plants expect a dry summer, they will tolerate moderate rain if the soil is well drained. Where summers are very wet, lift bulbs after leaves wither and store dry until autumn. Control mealy bugs, mites and aphids at first appearance.

■ **In pots:** lovely in pots and a good way to grow them where summers are wet or winters too cold. After flowering, stop watering and store the bulbs dry in their containers.

Lachenalia

Cape cowslip, Soldier boys

Family: *Liliaceae (Lily family).*
Type: *bulb.* **Native to:** *the western and south-western Cape region of South Africa but a few extend into the eastern part of the country. The climate is Mediterranean with most rain falling between mid-autumn and early spring. Around the Cape, some rain falls in summer, in other parts of the west coast, summers are nearly rainless. Lachenalias from the eastern parts of the country expect wet summers.*

■ **Preferred climate:** near frost-free, frost-free and subtropical gardens. Plants will accept frequent frosts down to -3°C (27°F) and odd extremes of -7°C (19°F). They are most hardy if given a hot, dry summer. In colder climates, grow in pots in a cool greenhouse.

■ **Planting tips:** plant in autumn 8cm (3in) deep, 10cm (4in) apart in well-drained soil in full sun. Where frosts are frequent you can plant them up to 15cm (6in) deep.

■ **Growing season:** autumn, winter and early spring. Flower stems stand about 30cm (12in) tall. In humid, frost-free areas where bulbs receive year-round rain, leaves are long and lank; in places where summers are drier and hotter and bulbs are baked dry, leaves are shorter and stiffer.

■ **Flowering season:** mid to late winter or early spring; greenhouse plants in cold climates usually flower in spring. Typical species have red-tipped, tubular yellow flowers; other species produce flowers in many lovely shades, including blue, lavender, white and pink; often beautiful combinations of these.

■ **Care:** ensure adequate moisture from the time growth begins until flowers fade. In well-drained soil, plants will tolerate moderate summer rain with no ill effect, apart from longer, lankier leaves. In heavy soils or where summers are very wet, lift bulbs after leaves wither, clean and store in just-damp vermiculite, sphagnum or peat until the following autumn.

■ **In pots:** ideal for window boxes or pots. Plant more shallowly and closely together than in the ground. Either lift bulbs after blooming or store dry in their pots.

*Below, left: Lachenalia carnosa **is a wonderful, showy species from the winter-rainfall south-west of South Africa.***

Below: *Lachenalia aloides **is the most widely known variety and one of the most spectacular.***

Leopoldia

(Syn. *Muscari comosum*), Plume hyacinth, Tassel hyacinth

Family: *Liliaceae (Lily family).* **Type:** *bulb.* **Native to:** *European and North African countries around the Mediterranean where the winters are cool to cold and rainy; the summers are warm to hot and vary, depending on the region, from virtually rainless to some rain.*

■ **Preferred climate:** cold, cool and near frost-free gardens. Plants are hardy to -40˚C (-40˚F) and do reasonably well where winter nights are in the 0-5˚C (32-41˚F) range.

■ **Planting tips;** plant in autumn 8cm (3in) deep, 13cm (5in) apart in good quality, well-drained soil in full sun. In frost-free areas plants will tolerate a few hours' light shade.

■ **Growing season:** autumn, winter and early spring or late winter and spring, the latter where winters are cool or cold. Plants reach a height of about 30cm (12in).

■ **Flowering season:** late winter to mid-spring, depending on the climate; the colder the climate, the later the flowers appear. The variety *Leopoldia comosa* 'Plumosum' is more attractive than the species.

■ **Care:** water after planting, if autumn is very dry. Plants form roots during the cool months and need soil moisture. When growth begins, give additional water; after blooming, let the plant dry out. When leaves begin to wither, they can be cut off. In well drained soils, plants will tolerate some summer rain but prefer dryness. In good conditions, bulbs multiply fast. Lift and separate clumps in summer.

■ **In pots:** not usually grown in pots as the leaves are somewhat untidy and the plants are easily grown in the garden.

Below: Leopoldia comosa **'Plumosum' is a fetching, feathery-flowered relative of the grape hyacinth.**

Leucocoryne

Glory of the sun

Family: *Amaryllidaceae (Hippeastrum family).* **Type:** *bulb.* **Native to:** *Chile, from sea level to 1000m (3300ft) where there is a Mediterranean climate. Almost all rain falls between mid-autumn and early spring. Frosts of -5˚C (23˚F) are possible in the highest parts but lowland areas are frost-free.*

■ **Preferred climate:** frost-free and near frost-free gardens, especially those with a Mediterranean climate. In colder climates, grow in pots in a greenhouse where winter night temperatures are above freezing. Outdoors, plants will accept occasional frosts of -2˚C (28˚F).

■ **Planting tips:** plant in autumn 5cm (2in) deep, 10cm (4in) apart in average, well-drained soil in full sun. In colder climates, they can be planted in late winter when frosts are light and almost finished.

■ **Growing season:** late autumn, winter and spring or, in colder climates, late winter, spring and early summer, to a height of about 30cm (12in). The grassy leaves are beginning to, or have, died back by the time the blue and white flowers appear in spring.

■ **Flowering season:** spring.

■ **Care:** water bulbs when you plant and, sparingly, until growth begins; then increase water but never keep the soil wet. Decrease when leaves begin to wither. Don't water during summer; bulbs expect dryness then and watering may cause rotting or disappointing flowers the following year. Plants are best grown in pots in summer rainfall zones.

■ **In pots:** plant more shallowly and closely together than in the garden. Keep moist and feed periodically with liquid organic plant food until leaves start to wither. Let pots dry out completely in summer.

Jack Hobbs / Photos Horticultural / Geoffrey Burnie

Above, top: Despite its beauty and ease of growth, Leucocoryne pupurea *is a rare bulb in warm-climate gardens.*

Above: Dainty Leucojum autumnale *is one of the prettiest of the genus. It flowers in early autumn.*

Inset, right: The common snowflake Leucojum aestivum *is always charming and easy to grow in cool or warm climates.*

Leucojum

Snowflake; sometimes called snowdrop in Australia and warmer parts of USA where the real snowdrop cannot be grown.

Family: *Amaryllidaceae (Hippeastrum family).* **Type:** *bulb.* **Native to:** *western Europe, Mediterranean Europe and North Africa, the Middle East where the winters are cool to near frost-free and rainy or snowy; the summers may be moderately rainy or fairly dry.*

■ **Preferred climate:** cool, near frost-free and frost-free gardens. In colder climates they can be grown in pots in cool greenhouses. Plants are generally hardy to -10°C (14°F).

■ **Planting tips:** plant late summer, 5cm (2in) deep and apart in a place where they can be left alone for years. *Leucojum vernum* and *L. aestivum* like rich, permanently moist soils and can take some shade. The pretty little autumn snowflake, *L. autumnale,* likes well-drained, rather sandy soil and full sun.

■ **Growing season:** autumn, winter and early spring to height of 30cm (12in).

■ **Flowering season:** autumn, for *L. autumnale* and *L. roseum,* or late winter/early spring. All species, except *L. roseum,* have white flowers.

■ **Care:** never allow *L. aestivum* or *L. vernum* to become dry. Conversely, take care not to overwater *L. autumnale.* Where rain falls year-round, the two former species usually need little attention.

■ **In pots:** *L. autumnale* and *L. roseum* are pretty enough to warrant pot culture. The others are not showy enough. Grow in wide, shallow containers and plant closely together for the best effect. Leave to dry out when dormant.

Lycoris

Spider lily

Family: *Amaryllidaceae (Hippeastrum family).* **Type:** *bulb.* **Native to:** *China, Japan, Taiwan where the winters are cool to frost-free. Rain falls in every month with summers, in some parts, being wetter than the winters.*

■ **Preferred climate:** cool, frost-free and subtropical gardens. In colder climates, they can be grown in pots with greenhouse protection. The hardiest species will tolerate -12°C (10°F), perhaps a little lower but plants generally do best where frosts are much less severe or unknown.

■ **Planting tips:** plant mid to late summer, with the tips of the bulbs just at, or under, the surface, or up to 10cm (4in) deep. The latter may be preferable where winters are frosty. Plant in well-drained but fertile and humus-rich soil in sun or part-shade.

■ **Growing season:** some species produce foliage immediately after the autumn flowers and grow through winter, while others do not grow leaves until late winter or early spring. *Lycoris incarnata* and *L. squamigera* are examples of the latter habit and these may be the

best choices where frosts are frequent and sharp. The golden spider lily, *L. aurea* has winter-growing leaves which are damaged by any other than the lightest of frosts.

■ **Flowering season:** late summer or early autumn. Flowers may be golden yellow, red or pink and stand up to 60cm (2ft) tall on thick, leafless stems.

■ **Care:** feed with complete plant food or slow-release fertiliser when leaves appear, then keep moist. While plants prefer dryness when dormant, moderate summer rain appears to have little effect on flowering if bulbs are grown in well-drained soil. Lycoris do not like to be lifted annually so, if summers are very wet or soils heavy, you can achieve the best results from pots which can be sheltered from rain.

■ **In pots:** plant closely together, not touching, and with the tips of the bulbs above the surface. Blend a small amount of slow-release fertiliser or complete plant food into the potting mix and, when leaves appear, feed monthly with a diluted solution of liquid organic fertiliser. Allow pots to dry when leaves wither.

Moraea

Peacock Iris

Family: *Iridaceae (Iris family).* **Type:** *corm.* **Native to:** *south-western Cape province, eastward to Natal and up the east coast of Africa to Ethiopia where the climate varies. In the south-west, from which the bulk of the species come, most rain falls between mid-autumn and early spring. Summers are warm to hot and with little rain. Further east and in tropical Africa, rain falls year-round but predominantly in the summer months. Inland and in highland parts, frosts of -10°C (14°F) are possible but are not common or prolonged.*

■ **Preferred climate:** cool, frost-free, subtropical and tropical gardens. In colder areas, raise summer-growing species in pots stored above freezing when dormant. Winter-growing species can also be grown in pots but in cold climates these will need frost-free winter nights and day temperatures of at least 10°C (50°F).

■ **Planting tips:** plant winter-growing species in autumn, summer growers and evergreens in late winter or early spring. Plant 5-8cm (2-3in) deep and space according to the mature size and spread of the plant – the biggest will need a 25cm (10in) spacing, the smallest, 5cm (2in). Plants enjoy deep, well-drained, sandy soil but any reasonably fertile, well-drained soil will do. Full sun is essential.

■ **Growing season:** autumn, winter and early spring or spring, summer and early autumn. Some are evergreen. Plants vary in height from about 15cm (6in) to over 1m (3ft).

■ **Flowering season:** those from winter rainfall areas (the winter growers) flower in late autumn, winter or early spring. Evergreens and summer growers bloom early to mid-summer. Different species produce flowers in a huge range of colours, often spotted or with contrasting centres. The genus gets its common name of peacock Iris from the iridescent blue blotch in the centres of the flowers of some species.

■ **Care:** water during the growing season is about all the regular maintenance these plants need. Watch for grasshoppers and protect from slugs, snails and spider mites. Species from the winter rainfall areas expect dry conditions in summer and will rot in warm, wet soils.

■ **In pots:** smaller species are especially suited to pots. Place corms closely together and feed monthly during the growing season.

Left page, top: The beautiful golden spider lily, Lycoris aurea, *produces flowers in early autumn. Luxuriant blue-green leaves follow.*

Right: Very easily grown, Moraea polystachya, *flowers abundantly during autumn with the odd flower continuing until spring.*

Inset, above: Moraea villosa *is one of the most beautiful and popular species. It comes in a variety of colours.*

Muscari

Grape hyacinth

Family: *Liliaceae (Lily family).*
Type: *bulb.* **Native to:** *European and North African countries around the Mediterranean where the winters are cool to cold and rainy; the summers warm to hot and varying, depending on the region, from virtually rainless to some rain.*

■ **Preferred climate:** cold, cool and near frost-free gardens. Plants are hardy to at least -30°C (-22°F) and do reasonably well where winter nights are in the 0-5°C (32-41°F) range.

■ **Planting tips:** plant in autumn 8cm (3in) deep and apart in good quality, well-drained soil in full sun or, where winters are barely frosty, light shade for part of the day.

■ **Growing season:** autumn, winter and early spring or late winter and spring, the latter where winters are cool to cold. Plants reach a height of about 20cm (8in).

■ **Flowering season:** late winter to mid-spring, depending on the climate; the colder the climate, the later the flowers appear.

■ **Care:** water after planting if autumn is dry. Plants form roots during the cool months and need soil moisture. When growth begins, give extra water but allow to dry out after blooming. When leaves begin to wither, they can be cut off or raked away. In well-drained soils, plants will accept some summer rain but prefer dryness. In good conditions, bulbs will multiply fast. Lift and separate clumps in summer.

■ **In pots:** *Muscari armeniacum* can be forced to flower early. Read the section titled "Forcing Bulbs to Bloom" on page 26 for details. It is a good bulb to use in conjunction with others suitable for forcing, such as hyacinths and tulips.

Above: Muscari armeniacum flowers in early spring and contrasts well with other early bloomers, such as these daffodils and jonquils.

Inset, above: Unusually shaped M. botryoides 'Album' from Central Europe has scented white flowers.

Right: M. neglectum has smaller heads of vibrant blue flowers. Its spreading habit makes it ideal for large scale naturalising.

Photos Horticultural

Narcissus

Daffodil, Jonquil, Narcissus

Family: *Amaryllidaceae (Hippeastrum family).* **Type:** *bulb.*
Native to: *southern Europe, especially Spain and Portugal, other Mediterranean countries in Europe and North Africa, western and central Asia, China and Japan from sea level to 3000m (9800ft). The climate there varies but winters are always at least cool, often very cold. Much of the area has a Mediterranean climate, i.e., wet winters, dry summers.*

■ **Preferred climate:** cold, cool and near frost-free gardens. Daffodils are hardy, well able to tolerate temperatures of -30°C (-34°F) but the tazetta types and those related to *Narcissus jonquilla* – usually called jonquils or Narcissus – are not as tough. They prefer to live where winter temperatures don't drop below -10°C (14°F). Like most spring-flowering, cold-climate bulbs, daffodils need cool soil in autumn to form roots. In frost-free and subtropical gardens, they often flower poorly even in their first season, because soil temperatures are too high. Even the multi-flowered jonquils, known to prefer warmer conditions, can find frost-free and subtropical gardens too warm to reliably reflower in subsequent years. Read the section titled "Soil Temperatures" on page 17 for more details on this subject.

■ **Planting tips:** plant early to mid-autumn (late summer in cold climates) 8-20cm (3-8in) deep – the deeper end of the range in warmer areas and in sandy soils – and 15cm (6in) apart, closer if bulbs will be lifted after blooming. Any fertile, well-drained soil suits. Drop a light sprinkling of complete plant food into the planting hole, cover with 5cm (2in) of soil and place bulb on top. Full sun is best for all types in winter and early spring but those which flower late in spring will appreciate the shade cast by the emerging leaves of deciduous trees or shrubs.

■ **Growing season:** late winter, spring and early summer to a height of 30cm (12in) or less.

■ **Flowering season:** from late autumn to late spring depending on the species. Flower colours are mostly in shades of yellow but there are pink and white varieties and many bi-colours.

■ **Care:** keep moist from the time growth begins until after flowers finish. When shoots first appear, feed with soluble or liquid plant food and again when flower buds are seen. Don't remove any foliage until it has yellowed. If necessary, lift bulbs when growth withers and store clean and dry in a dark, cool, airy place until the following autumn.

■ **In pots:** one of the best bulbs for potting and the only way to grow them in warm areas. Potted bulbs need about 10 weeks of chilling to form roots. In cold climates, this can be achieved outside in autumn. In warm climates, refrigerate the potted bulbs. After chilling period, keep pot cool. Read the section titled "Heatstroke Danger" on page 26.

Right: Blossom trees and bulbs are two of the strongest symbols of spring. Here, a cherry tree underplanted with daffodils makes a brilliant display.

Below, from left: Jonquils have fragrant flowers in clusters atop each stem. Here are Narcissus tazetta *plus the hybrids 'Soleil d'or' and 'Paperwhite';* N. romieuxii; *N.* 'Rip van Winkle'; *N. cyclamineus; N.* 'Duet'; *N. bulbocodium,* the hoop petticoat daffodil.

Leigh Clapp / Lorna Rose / Photos Horticultural

Nerine

Guernsey lily

Family: *Amaryllidaceae (Hippeastrum family).* **Type:** *bulb.* **Native to:** *a wide area of southern Africa but most species come from the summer rainfall areas of eastern South Africa, at elevations of up to 3000m (9800ft). There are also species from the winter rainfall area of the south-west. The climate over the total area varies from rain in winter, to rain in summer, to rain year-round. Winters are mild to warm, depending on the altitude.*

■ **Preferred climate:** cool, frost-free and subtropical gardens. Can be grown in pots everywhere. *Nerine bowdenii* is the hardiest species, able to tolerate extreme lows of -15˚C (5˚F), perhaps -20˚C (-4˚F) but not for long periods and not when the soil is also wet. If such temperatures are possible, plant deeply at the foot of a wall that faces the sun. Other species will tolerate the odd light frost only.

■ **Planting tips:** plant winter-growing species in late summer, summer-growing species in early spring. Plant with necks of bulbs at or just below the surface or with as much as 13cm (5in) of soil over them – the latter is probably best in cooler climates. Nerines demand good drainage and do well in sandy or gravelly soil in full sun. Once planted, most species like to be left where they are.

■ **Growing season:** some species flower in early autumn, then produce their leaves and grow through winter, dying back in summer for a dry rest. Others are dormant in winter and grow during summer or are evergreen. Most are under 60cm (2ft) tall.

■ **Flowering season:** white or shades of pink or red. All species flower in late summer or autumn. After initial planting or replanting following lifting, flowers may not appear for a year or two.

■ **Care:** water during the growing season if rain does not fall. Nerines like moisture but not a lot of water. They can be fed when leaves appear but, if the soil is reasonably fertile, this is not necessary. When dormant, keep plants as dry as possible.

■ **In pots:** especially lovely when packed together in pots. Plant with necks just above soil level. In cold climates, bring potted plants into a frost-free greenhouse when low temperatures threaten.

Photos Horticultural / Jack Hobbs / Brent Wilson / Geoffrey Burnie

Ornithogalum

Chincherinchee, Star of Bethlehem

Family: *Liliaceae (Lily family).*
Type: *bulb.* **Native to:** *UK and northern Europe, Mediterranean Europe, western Asia and southern Africa where the climate varies from cold and snowy to frost-free winters. Rain may fall year-round or only in winter. The southern African species are the least hardy, those from northern Europe are the hardiest.*

■ **Preferred climate:** cold, cool, frost-free and subtropical gardens, depending on the species. The hardiest will tolerate -20°C (4°F), the most tender accept no frost at all.

■ **Planting tips:** in frost-free or near-frost free areas, plant in autumn. In colder climates, bulbs native to Europe can also be planted in autumn but South African bulbs are planted in spring for summer flowering and lifted in autumn. Plant bulbs 5-8cm (2-3in) deep. Spacing depends on the ultimate size of the plant. For low growers, 10cm (4in)

is the acceptable distance, but the larger species should have 30cm (12in) between them. Deep, sandy, very well drained soil is ideal and a position in full sun is essential.

■ **Growing season:** autumn, winter and early spring or spring, summer and early autumn depending on the species. Popular species grow to 60cm (2ft) or less.

■ **Flowering season:** late winter to late summer, depending on the species. South African species have white or coloured flowers; those from other areas are white only.

■ **Care:** start watering when leaves appear and keep evenly moist until after blooming. Plants can multiply fast. Lift and separate clumps when overcrowded – every 2-3 years.

■ **In pots:** leaves are generally too coarse and massive for pot culture but both *Ornithogalum arabicum* and *O. thyrsoides* are sometimes grown under glass in cooler climates for their long-lasting flowers.

Left, top: The pretty pink-flowering Nerine bowdenii *is the hardiest species and one of the most popular.*

Left, bottom: Bright and startling, Nerine fothergillii 'Major' *produces its fiery orange-red flowers in early autumn.*

Above: Chincherinchee, Ornithogalum thyrsoides, *is an alluring, long-lasting cut flower, although it is not hardy.*

Inset, above: The beautiful blooms of Ornithogalum arabicum *make it a favourite choice for sunny garden beds in mild areas.*

Oxalis

Family: *Oxalidaceae (Oxalis family).* **Type:** *bulb or tuber.* ***Native to:*** *very wide distribution but most are found in tropical and subtropical South America and in South Africa where the climate varies.*

■ **Preferred climate:** cool and frost-free gardens. Some species are hardy to -15˚C (5˚F), others tolerate little or no frost. In cold climates, they must be given the warmth and shelter of a greenhouse. In all climates, untried species of Oxalis are often viewed as potential weeds and kept in containers to evaluate their performance. Only when you are satisfied that the plant will not spread in your climate should you consider garden planting. As it happens, Oxalis make charming container plants and are happy to live in pots indefinitely.

■ **Planting tips:** plant winter-growing species in late summer, summer growers in early spring, about 3cm (1in) deep and 8-15cm (3-6in) apart. Plants from South Africa's dry south-west demand good drainage and do well in sandy soils. Those from tropical South America also need good drainage but prefer soils that are more humus-rich and fertile.

Brent Wilson / Jack Hobbs / Photos Horticultural

■ **Growing season:** autumn, winter and spring, or spring, summer and early autumn, depending on the species. Bulbous and tuberous Oxalis are generally low, rounded plants.

■ **Flowering season:** autumn, winter, spring and summer, depending on the species. Flowers may be white, yellow, apricot, pink or red. Flowers open only in sun.

■ **Care:** winter-growing species are largely from South Africa's dry south-west and, while they need water during autumn and winter, they do not like to be over-watered. Allow the soil to nearly dry out between waterings. Species from rainy and humid tropical South America need plenty of water during their summer-growing season and high humidity. All species can be fed lightly, monthly with liquid organic fertiliser. When leaves begin to die back, reduce watering. Keep dry when dormant.

■ **In pots:** a good and safe way to grow all species. The plants look terrific in wide, shallow containers on sunny tables or as spot colour in the garden.

*Left, top: **Richly coloured** Oxalis tetraphylla **syn.** O. deppei, **from Mexico, flowers late summer. It tolerates light frosts only.***

*Far left, bottom: **An unusual container plant,** O. massoniana **is winter growing and flowers in late autumn and early winter.***

*Left, bottom: **Pretty** O. adenophylla, **from the mountains of Chile and Argentina, grows in spring and summer, flowering in early summer.***

Puschkinia

Family: *Liliaceae (Lily family).*
Type: *bulb.* **Native to:** *mountains of Turkey, Lebanon, Caucasus region, commonly near the snowline and at altitudes of up to 3000m (9800ft). The winters there are severe, with temperatures down to at least -30˚C (-22˚F). Bulbs are usually snow-covered in winter and are brought into growth by melt-water in spring. Summers are cool and relatively dry.*

■ **Preferred climate:** cold and cool-climate gardens. Rarely offered in warm climates as the bulbs require at least 12 weeks at 4˚C (40˚F) for root formation.

■ **Plant:** in autumn 5-10cm (2-4in) deep and 10-15cm (4-6in) apart in gravelly, well-drained soil that has enough peat or humus to retain some moisture. Full sun is essential. Plants do not enjoy frequent lifting so site them where they can be left undisturbed.

■ **Grows:** spring and summer to a height of about 20cm (8in).

■ **Flowers:** in spring. Flowers are a soft, baby blue.

■ **Care:** keep moist from late winter until after flowers fade. Allow to nearly dry out in summer but remember, in their mountainous homelands, some moisture is always available.

■ **In pots:** an excellent pot plant when crowded together, the hyacinth-like flowers offer a good display. They must be exposed to near freezing temperatures for 12 weeks to form roots. Bring indoors when flower stems are well formed.

*Below: **Enchanting** Puschkinia scilloides **syn.** P. libanotica **is for cool to cold climates only.***

Rhodohypoxis

Family: *Hypoxidaceae (Hypoxis family).* **Type:** *rhizome.* **Native to:** *mountains of eastern South Africa at altitudes of between 1200-2500m (4000-7000ft) in damp, peaty soaks in grassy areas. The winters there are relatively dry but always frosty and often snowy with temperatures falling to at least -10°C (14°F). Plants are brought into growth by spring melt-water, rain and frequent cool mists. Summers are cool and rainy.*

■ **Preferred climate:** cool and near frost-free gardens. Can be grown in containers in colder climates if given greenhouse shelter in winter. Plants will tolerate -10°C (14°F) but not if the soil is wet. From high alpine areas, they are not suited to humid, frost-free or subtropical gardens.

■ **Planting tips:** plant in autumn 3cm (1in) deep and 8cm (3in) apart in full sun. If temperatures are likely to fall below -7°C (19°F), 10cm (4in) of mulch should be applied as a protective layer. Scrape it away in late winter when nights are warmer but before growth begins. Plants will not tolerate cold, wet soil. During

Ranunculus

Family: *Ranunculaceae (Ranunculus family).* **Type:** *tuber.* **Native to:** *Asia Minor where the climate is Mediterranean, with wet winters and relatively dry summers.*

■ **Preferred climate:** cold, cool and frost-free gardens. The tubers are not particularly hardy but, in cold climates, they may be planted in spring for late spring and summer blooms; in warmer climates they are planted in autumn for late winter and spring blooms.

■ **Planting tips:** in frost-free and near frost-free areas, plant tubers mid-autumn for blooms in late winter or early spring. In cooler climates, spring planting, after frosts, gives late spring and early summer flowers. Where summers are not very hot, tubers may also be planted later in spring for late summer blooms. Plant in moist, friable, well-drained soil 3cm (1in) deep and about 20cm (8in) apart. The claws of the tubers should point downwards.

■ **Growing season:** winter and spring or spring and summer, depending on when they are planted. Plants grow to about 40cm (16in) in height.

■ **Flowering season:** late winter, early spring or late spring and summer. Flowers may be white, yellow, orange, pink or red.

■ **Care:** add complete plant food before planting and plant in moist soil. Keep lightly moist until growth begins, then increase the water. After blooming, pull up and discard plants as tubers are not worth the effort of saving – Ranunculus are one of the most inexpensive bulbs.

■ **In pots:** Ranunculus give a pretty display in pots but it is important to shade the sides of the pot from direct sun. Read the section titled "Heatstroke Danger" on page 26.

extended rain periods in winter, protect the dormant bulbs with a pane of glass. In gardens, Rhodohypoxis are best suited to small rockery pockets or alpine beds.

■ **Growing season:** spring and summer. All species are widespreading plants, barely 8cm (3in) tall.

■ **Flowering season:** late spring and early summer in white, pink or red.

■ **Care:** keep relatively dry in winter but lightly moisten soil in early spring whether growth is visible or not. As growth proceeds, gradually increase water but don't keep sodden. Feed with liquid organic fertiliser when growth begins, then more during the season. Decrease watering towards the end of summer.

■ **In pots:** possibly the best way to enjoy these plants. Use a gravelly mix which contains enough peat to keep the mix moist. Grow in an alpine house or a cool greenhouse and keep fairly dry over winter. Feed by blending a small ration of slow release fertiliser with the potting mix.

Rhodophiala

Family: *Amaryllidaceae (Hippeastrum family).* **Type:** *bulb.* **Native to:** *Andean Chile, Argentina and Bolivia and also Uruguay and north-eastern Argentina where the climate is generally warm year-round. Winters are near frost-free in the hills and frost-free closer to the coast. Rainfall is higher in summer than in winter but winters are not completely dry.*

■ **Preferred climate:** near frost-free, frost-free, subtropical and tropical gardens. In colder climates, grow in pots in heated greenhouses as for Hippeastrum. Bulbs should tolerate light frosts, not below -5°C (23°F), if protected by a layer of mulch.

■ **Planting tips:** plant in late summer or autumn in well-drained soil containing a lot of rotted organic matter. Plant bulbs with their tips at soil level. Where frosts are likely, lay 8cm (3in) of mulch over the top. Space about 10cm (4in) apart. Full sun is the best aspect, except in hot climates where some light shade in the afternoon is helpful. Choose a site where plants can be left undisturbed.

■ **Growing season:** in spring, summer and autumn to about 30cm (12in) tall.

■ **Flowering season:** in summer in orange, red, pink or cream, depending on the species.

■ **Care:** give water when growth begins, gradually increasing it as plants grow and summer approaches. Apply complete plant food when growth begins or feed monthly with liquid organic fertiliser.

■ **In pots:** pretty in pots, like slimmed down Hippeastrums, but choose a deep container. Plant bulbs 5cm (2in) apart with their tips exposed. In colder climates, give greenhouse protection until days and nights are frost-free. Maintain night temperatures above freezing and keep pots very lightly moist until growth begins.

Far left, top: Ranunculus asiaticus is the parent of today's modern hybrids which are double-flowered and multi-coloured.

Left, bottom: Rhodohypoxis has been extensively hybridised and there are numerous colour varieties. This one is called 'Stella'.

Above: Rhodophiala chilense has flowers in various colours which are produced in a long succession over summer.

Scilla

Squill

Family: *Liliaceae (Lily family)*.
Type: *bulb*. **Native to:** *central and western Europe, Mediterranean Europe, northern and southern Africa where the climate varies widely from cool to tropical.*

■ **Preferred climate:** tropical to cool-climate gardens, depending on the species. The hardiest will tolerate -20°C (4°F), while the most tender are best in frost-free areas.

■ **Planting tips:** plant in autumn, 8cm (3in) deep and about 15cm (6in) apart – wider for the bigger species. Best soil is humus-rich and sandy but average, well-drained soil will do. Full sun generally suits but in hotter areas, dappled or partial shade can be better.

■ **Growing season:** in spring, summer and early autumn. Height and spread depends on the species but most are under 45cm (18in).

■ **Flowering season:** in spring or summer, depending on the species, in various shades of blue.

■ **Care:** moisture must be available from the time plants start to grow until leaves begin to yellow. If soil is humus-rich and mulched when plants are dormant, no additional feeding is necessary.

■ **In pots:** worthwhile growing in pots as the blue flowers can be showy. The smaller-growing species are the most suitable.

Above: The satin-textured Romulea leipoldii, from the south-west of South Africa, looks pretty in pots.

Right: Scilla peruviana is an outstanding, near-evergreen summer-flowering species.

Inset, right: Siberian squill, S. siberica, tolerates severe frosts and makes a terrific pot or garden plant in cool climates.

Romulea

Onion grass, Satin flower

Family: *Iridaceae.* **Type:** *corm.*
Native to: *southern UK to Mediterranean Europe, Turkey, Lebanon and South Africa where the climate varies, but generally winters are rainy or snowy and summers warm to hot and relatively dry.*

■ **Preferred climate:** cool and near frost-free gardens, especially those with a Mediterranean climate. European and Middle Eastern species are the hardiest, able to tolerate at least -10°C (14°F). South African species are less cold tolerant but most should be safe to -5°C (23°F). In cold climates, grow in pots sheltered in a frost-free greenhouse. They are generally not successful in humid, frost-free areas.

■ **Planting tips:** plant in autumn, 5cm (2in) deep, and the same distance apart, in gravelly, well-drained soil that contains enough organic matter to retain some moisture. Full sun is essential.

■ **Growing season:** late winter and spring to 15-20cm (6-8in) tall.

■ **Flowering season:** in spring or early summer but only on sunny days for a few hours around midday. The satin-textured flowers come in many colours.

■ **Care:** consistent moisture during autumn, winter and spring is essential but, plants should be dried out as summer approaches, then kept as dry as possible for the season. Where summers are rainy, plants may rot unless covered with a sheet of glass.

■ **In pots:** Pretty in pots, especially wide, shallow containers. In cold climates, keep in a frost-free greenhouse in full sun. Store bulbs dry over summer in their containers and don't unpot and separate until overcrowding is affecting flowering.

Sparaxis

Harlequin flower

Family: *Iridaceae (Iris family).*
Type: *corm.* **Native to:** *Cape province of South Africa which has a Mediterranean climate with most rain falling between mid-autumn and early spring. Summers are much more dry.*

■ **Preferred climate:** Near frost-free, frost-free and subtropical gardens. In colder climates, grow in containers in a frost-free greenhouse in full sun. Plants will tolerate -5°C (23°F) but not frequently and not for long periods.

■ **Planting tips:** plant in autumn, 5cm (2in) deep, 10cm (4in) apart in fertile soil that drains freely. Full sun is essential.

■ **Growing season:** autumn, winter and early spring to about 25cm (10in) or less. Foliage develops into a neat fan.

■ **Flowering season:** in early spring. Some species have contrasting centres, the colour outlined and segmented in black.

■ **Care:** moisture during the growing season is about all these easy bulbs require. They prefer dryness in summer but if soil drains well, moderate summer rain will be harmless. If prolonged wet weather is likely in summer, lift and store bulbs when foliage dies back.

■ **In pots:** excellent pot subjects and, in cold climates, this is the only way to grow them. Plant corms more closely together. In cold climates, grow in a greenhouse kept frost-free at night and about 10°C (50°F) during the day. When bulbs are dormant they may be stored in their pots. Don't separate until overcrowding affects flowering.

Spiloxene

Midday stars

Family: *Hypoxidaceae (Hypoxis family).* **Type:** *corm.* **Native to:** *western and southern South Africa which has a Mediterranean climate with wet winters and warm to hot, fairly dry summers.*

■ **Preferred climate:** frost-free, near frost-free and cool climate gardens. Plants are winter-growing but are not able to tolerate deep freezes or even long periods of near freezing weather. They will accept -10°C (14°F) occasionally and lighter frosts more frequently. In cold climates, try planting the bulbs at the end of winter when frosts have almost gone to achieve blooming in late spring. Lift the bulbs when they become dormant in summer and store above freezing until late in the following winter.

■ **Planting tips:** in autumn in dense masses, 5cm (2in) deep, 8-10cm (3-4in) apart in average, well-drained soil in full sun.

■ **Growing season:** autumn, winter and early spring or, if planted after winter's end in a cold climate, during spring and summer. Plants are generally small, growing to a height of less than 25cm (10in).

■ **Flowering season:** mid-winter to mid-spring depending on the species – or late spring in cold places. Flowers only open on sunny days and come in white or shades of yellow and pink. The flowering season is relatively short.

■ **Care:** give plenty of water for the first few weeks after growth appears, then gradually taper off as summer approaches. When leaves begin to wither, stop watering. Plants enjoy a hot, dry summer but they will tolerate moderate summer rain if soil drains well.

■ **In pots:** best in wide containers where a massed effect can be achieved. In cold climates, shelter the pots in a greenhouse kept frost-free at night in autumn and winter and rising to 10°C (50°F) during the day.

Left, clockwise from top left: a mass of Sparaxis grandiflora; Sparaxis hybrids; the most popular species, Sparaxis tricolor, seen here with forget-me-nots; hybrid flowers can vary widely.

Above: Eye-catching Spiloxene capensis is the most widely grown species. Flower colour varies from white to yellow.

Sternbergia

Autumn daffodil, Autumn Crocus

Family: *Amaryllidaceae (Hippeastrum family).* **Type:** *bulb.* **Native to:** *Mediterranean Europe from Spain to Turkey. Also the Middle East, Caucasus, Iran and Kashmir. The climate there is Mediterranean with cold to cool winters that are rainy or snowy followed by hot, rainless, or near rainless summers.*

■ **Preferred climate:** cold, cool and near frost-free gardens. Possible in cool spots in frost-free areas. With the protection of a layer of mulch, or planted against a sunny wall, bulbs are hardy to -23°C (-10°F). In all situations they need a hot, fairly dry summer to succeed.

■ **Planting tips:** plant mid to late summer, 15cm (6in) deep – deeper in colder climates – and about 10cm (4in) apart. Average, well-drained soil will do, in full sun. While the bulbs are tolerant of alkaline soils (pH 7.5-8), as sometimes found in their natural habitats, they will grow in a more acidic environment.

■ **Growing season:** autumn, winter and early spring in mild climates; spring and early summer in colder places. All species are low plants, usually under 20cm (8in).

■ **Flowering season:** in early autumn except for *Sternbergia fischeriana* and *S. candida* which flower in early spring. Flowers are yellow or white.

■ **Care:** give moisture but not wetness in autumn. When frosts begin, reduce watering so that soil is kept just damp. Water can be increased again for a few weeks in early spring but, as summer approaches, let the bulbs go dry. Bulbs expect a hot, dry summer but if soil drains very freely, moderate summer water will not harm.

■ **In pots:** charming potted plants and a good way to grow them if your summers are rainy.

Synnotia

Family: *Iridaceae (Iris family).* **Type:** *corm.* **Native to:** *south-west of South Africa which has a Mediterranean climate with rainy, near frost-free winters and hot, relatively dry summers.*

■ **Preferred climate:** near frost-free, frost-free and subtropical gardens. Plants will accept occasional light frosts but are not for areas that experience long freezes or long periods of near-freezing temperatures.

■ **Planting tips:** plant in big groups in late summer, 5cm (2in) deep, 10cm (4in) apart into moist, sandy, well-drained soil in full sun.

■ **Growing season:** autumn, winter and spring. Mature height varies with species between 25-60cm (10-24in). Plants have erect, sword-shaped leaves.

■ **Flowering season:** mid to late spring.

■ **Care:** plant into moist soil and keep soil moist until leaves begin to wither in late spring. Complete plant food or slow-release fertiliser can be given when leaves appear. Don't

Photos Horticultural

water at all during summer. Where summers are wet, lift bulbs when foliage dies back and store them dry until late summer.

■ **In pots:** possible but choose wide, fairly deep tubs as a big clump is necessary for a good display. In cold climates, grow potted bulbs in a greenhouse kept above freezing at night and about 10°C (50°F) during the day. Bulbs can be kept in their pots for at least two seasons.

Left: Charming and small, Sternbergia lutea **is the most popular variety. It flowers in early autumn.**

Above: Synnotia villosa **produces lots of pretty, small flowers and gives the best display in drifts.**

Right: For the best display, crowd pretty, intensely coloured **Chilean Crocus,** Tecophilaea cyanocrocus, **in pots.**

Tecophilaea

Chilean Crocus

Family: *Tecophilaeaceae (Tecophilaea family).* **Type:** *corm.* **Native to:** *high levels of the Chilean Andes where the climate is cold but bulbs are protected by snow cover and are brought into growth by spring melt-water. Summers are cool and there is always some moisture in the soil.*

■ **Preferred climate:** cold, cool and near frost-free gardens. Not suited to humid, frost-free areas. In cool and cold climates, it is usually grown in pots in cool greenhouses.

■ **Planting tips:** plant in autumn in a humus-rich but gritty and well-drained soil. Plant corms 5cm (2in) deep, 10cm (4in) apart in either full sun or where there is some dappled shade from early afternoon. Choose a site where the bulbs can be left alone for years.

■ **Growing season:** late autumn, winter and spring to about 15cm (6in) tall.

■ **Flowering season:** late winter to late spring, depending on the climate – the cooler the climate, the later the flowers appear. Flowers are an intense blue with or without a white eye.

■ **Care:** plant in damp soil in autumn and water only if there is a risk of the soil drying out. In near frost-free climates, water can be increased after mid-winter and, when growth begins, keep moist. Reduce water at the start of summer. Where summers are rainy, bulbs will need protection from excess water and should be covered.

■ **In pots:** this is the best way to grow them. In cool and cold climates, shelter pots in a greenhouse kept frost-free at night, especially if growth has begun in autumn as sharp frosts will damage the leaves. Keep evenly moist while growing but ease off watering as summer approaches.

Trillium

**Wake robin, Birth root,
Lamb's quarters**

Family: *Liliaceae (Lily family).*
Type: *rhizome.* **Native to:** *North
America, Japan, north-east Asia,
Himalayas where winters are cool to
very cold, often snowy; the summers
mild to warm and rainy.*

■ **Preferred climate:** cold, cool
and near frost-free gardens. From
cool, moist, deciduous forests,
plants are hardy to severe frosts and
snow but will not succeed where
winter minimums are above freezing.

■ **Planting tips:** plant in autumn
in deep, moist, acidic soil that is rich
in rotted organic matter. Plant
rhizomes 10-15cm (4-6in) deep and
about 30cm (12in) apart. Plants accept
late autumn and winter sun but must
have shade from about mid-spring on.
They do not enjoy a hot position,
even if it is well watered.

■ **Growing season:** late winter
to early summer. Mature height
varies from about 10cm (4in) to over
60cm (2ft), depending on the species.

■ **Flowering season:** mid to
late spring or early summer in white,
cream, pinks or purples.

■ **Care:** leave undisturbed when
established. Most water is needed
when plants are growing but some
moisture is needed at all times. If
soil is fertile and mulched with
fallen leaves every year, no other
feeding is necessary.

■ **In pots:** possible, but choose a
wide pot that will hold at least three
plants. Feed monthly with liquid
organic fertiliser from the time
growth appears and never allow to
dry out. The smaller-growing
species are probably the best
choices for containers.

Triteleia

Family: *Liliaceae (Lily family).*
Type: *corm.* **Native to:** *western USA
which has a Mediterranean climate,
with most rain falling from late
autumn to early spring. Decreasing
rain falls from mid-spring to
mid-summer with little or none in
late summer and early autumn.*

■ **Preferred climate:** cool, near
frost-free and frost-free gardens.
Plants accept -10°C (14°F) if
protected by a layer of mulch but
exposure to this type of temperature
should be short-lived.

■ **Planting tips:** plant in late
summer or early autumn, in big
groups, 15cm (6in) deep, 10cm (4in)
apart. Deep, sandy soil with some
organic content is best but any
well-drained, reasonably fertile soil
will do. After planting, cover bulbs
with a 5cm (2in) layer of mulch —
more if low temperatures are

expected in winter – but scrape deep layers back before growth begins. Full sun is essential.

■ **Growing season:** winter, spring and early summer to a height of about 30cm (12in).

■ **Flowering season:** late spring to early summer, usually after the leaves have died away. Flowers are blue-mauve.

■ **Care:** start watering the site in late autumn and keep moist until leaves begin to wither. Once established, do not disturb plants.

■ **In pots:** possible in pots but dead and dying leaves at flowering time detract from the effect; these can be trimmed. Store bulbs dry in their pots over summer. Don't unpot or separate for at least two seasons.

Tritonia

Blazing star

Family: *Iridaceae (Iris family).*
Type: *corm.* **Native to:** *tropical and southern Africa. Most species are native to the southern Cape Province of South Africa. Their native climate is warm to hot year-round. Winters here are wet and lightly frosty; the summers with slight rainfalls. Plants from this climate grow during the cooler months and remain dormant in summer. In other areas rain falls year-round or is concentrated in summer. Plants have a summer-growing, winter-dormant habit.*

■ **Preferred climate:** cool, frost-free and subtropical gardens. In colder climates, the winter-growing plants may be held back for planting in early spring for late spring and summer bloom. There are also a few summer-growing species which suit colder climates. In the wild, winter-growing Tritonia experience frosts of -5°C (23°F), possibly lower but they are not hardy to extended periods of below-freezing weather.

■ **Planting tips:** plant winter-growing species in autumn, summer-growers in spring. In cold climates, all species may be planted in late winter or early spring, a few weeks before frosts have finished. Plant 5cm (2in) deep, 8cm (3in) apart in fertile, free-draining soil in full sun.

■ **Growing season:** autumn, winter and spring, or spring, summer and early autumn, depending on the species. Mature height varies but most are under 60cm (2ft).

■ **Flowering season:** winter-growers flower from late winter to late spring, depending on species; summer-growers from early summer to early autumn. Flower colour varies, depending on the species, from cream, yellow, orange and pink to red.

■ **Care:** ensure adequate moisture during the growing season but allow corms to dry out after blooming. Plants will tolerate moderate rainfall during their dormant state but only if soil drains fast. Where summers are wet, lift winter-growing species after leaves wither and store dry over summer. In cold climates, lift all types after the first frost and store dry, above freezing until the following spring.

■ **In pots:** possible. Greenhouse owners in cold climates can raise winter-growing species in containers kept above freezing at night and about 10°C (50°F) during the day.

Far left, top: These terrific double flowers are produced by Trillium grandiflorum **'Flore Pleno'.**

Far left, bottom: Trillium grandiflorum **'Roseum'** *has soft pink flowers.*

Left: Triteleia laxa **'Queen Fabiola'** *is one of the most attractive types available.*

Above, left: Elegant hybrid Tritonias like this one are the most commonly grown.

Above, right: Delicately patterned, winter-growing Tritonia squalida *takes light frosts and flowers in early spring.*

Tulipa

Tulip

Family: *Liliaceae (Lily family).*
Type: *bulb.* **Native to:** *the Caucasus region, Turkmenistan, Central Asia where winters are very cold, often snowy, followed by short, moist springs and long, hot, dry summers. Total rainfall is relatively low.*

■ **Preferred climate:** cold, cool and near frost-free gardens. Possible in pots in warmer areas but potted bulbs will need refrigeration. Tulips are hardy to -40°C (-40°F) but are rarely successful where winters are frost-free, even in their first year.

■ **Planting tips:** plant mid to late autumn. Tulips need cool soil – under 11°C (52°F) – to form roots and shouldn't be planted too early in autumn. Read the sections titled "Soil Temperature" on page 17 and "Refrigerating Bulbs" on page 8 for more details. Plant bulbs 10-20cm (4-8in) deep in deeply dug, humus-rich, well-drained soil, spacing them 10-15cm apart. The deeper plantings are recommended in sandy soils or in areas that are the least frosty. Tulips must have full sun and prefer higher or sloping ground to frost-collecting hollows.

■ **Growing season:** late winter, spring and early summer, up to a height of about 30cm (12in).

■ **Flowering season:** late winter to mid-spring. There are early, mid and late season bloomers available, so it is possible to have an extended tulip season. Flowers come in every colour except blue and green.

■ **Care:** drop bulb food or complete plant food in the base of the planting hole, cover with 5cm (2in) of soil and place bulb on top. Water in and ensure that soil stays moist, but not too wet, during autumn and winter. At first sign of growth, feed with liquid or soluble plant food, then again when flower buds appear. Keep soil evenly moist whenever leaves are present. Allow leaves to die off naturally before removing. In cold climates, *species* tulips can be left in the ground over summer provided that that season is not too wet. The plants expect heat and dryness for at least the last two months of summer. Everywhere, *hybrid* tulips should be lifted after leaves wither, cleaned and stored in a cool, dark, airy place over summer. Where winters are not very cold, *species* tulips should also be treated this way.

■ **In pots:** splendid pot plants but remember their chilling requirements. You should also read the section titled "Bulbs in Pots" on page 24. Plant bulbs closely together, but not touching. Tulip bulbs have a flat side and this should face towards the outside of the pot. The first leaf, which is big and broad, will grow in that direction and not congest the centre of the pot. Plant so that the tips of the bulbs are at, or just under, the surface. In cold climates, potted bulbs can be planted in the garden after blooming but elsewhere they are best discarded. They will not reflower in pots in the following year.

Above, from left: Iran's Tulipa urumiensis; *a double-flowered hybrid 'Angelique'; bi-coloured* T. clusiana *'Cynthia'.*

Right, top: One of the world's loveliest flowers, over two billion hybrid tulips are planted every year.

Right, below, from left: Tulipa fosteriana *'Candela'; the lily-flowered tulip 'Alladin'; robust and early-flowering,* T. turkestanica *from Central Asia.*

Photos Horticultural / Geoffrey Burnie / Leigh Clapp / Lorna Rose / Andrew Henley-Auscape

Veltheimia

Veldt lily

Family: *Liliaceae (Lily family).*
Type: *bulb.* **Native to:** *South Africa.
Two species:* **Veltheimia capensis***,
is native to the winter-rainfall,
largely frost-free south-west of South
Africa;* **Veltheimia bracteata** *is
from the south-east of that country
which experiences year-round rain
and little or no frost.*

■ **Preferred climate:** near
frost-free, frost-free and tropical
gardens. In colder climates plants
are easily raised in pots if given the
shelter of a greenhouse kept
frost-free at night and between
10-15˚C (50-59˚F) during the day.
They can be placed outdoors when
frosts are finished.

■ **Planting tips:** plant mid to late
summer with the neck and
shoulders of the bulb above ground
level. Good drainage is essential.
Any reasonably fertile soil will do.
Veltheimia capensis accepts more
sun than *V. bracteata* but both
species enjoy shade during the
hottest hours of the day. Plants do
not appreciate annual lifting so site
where they can be left alone.

■ **Growing season:** *V. capensis*
grows mid-autumn, winter and early
spring; *V. bracteata* is evergreen or
nearly evergreen, sometimes lying
dormant for a month or two in early
summer if that season is dry. Plants
grow to about 60cm (2ft) tall.

■ **Flowering season:** *V.
capensis* flowers late autumn to
early winter; *V. bracteata* is in
bloom mid-winter to early spring.
Flowers are a dusty pink.

■ **Care:** Both species need water
when they are in leaf. *V. capensis*
likes to be kept dry in summer.
Where summers are wet, grow
V. bracteata. Neither needs
regular feeding if soil is reasonably
fertile. Snails and slugs are attracted
to leaves.

■ **In pots:** excellent pot plants;
both species will tolerate life in
dim interiors for a few weeks at a
time. In cold climates, grow in a
tub in the greenhouse or in a
warm, bright room.

Watsonia

Family: *Iridaceae (Iris family).*
Type: *corm.* **Native to:** *western,
south-western and eastern South
Africa where the climate varies from
Mediterranean in the west and
south-west – that is, wet winters,
with hot, relatively dry summers –
to humid and subtropical in the
east with year-round rain most
heavy in summer.*

■ **Preferred climate:** near
frost-free, frost-free and subtropical
gardens. Spring and summer-
growing species may be grown in
colder climates if lifted in autumn.
Most species are winter growers.
While they will tolerate frosts of
-5˚C (23˚F), they do not like
continuously cold weather.

■ **Planting tips:** plant
winter-growing, spring-flowering
species in autumn; summer-growing

Nancy Gardiner/John Carnemolla/Australian Picture Library/Jack Hobbs

and evergreen species in early spring when frosts, if any, are almost gone. Plant 10-15cm (4-6in) deep, 15-20cm (6-8in) apart in any reasonably fertile soil. In frost-free areas, winter-growing species will tolerate soils that are wet in winter; other species prefer good drainage. Full sun is best, except in hot climates where some shade in the afternoon is preferred.

■ **Growing season:** autumn, winter and early spring, or spring and summer. Some plants are evergreeen. Most are winter growing. Plants vary in height from about 35cm (14in) to over 1.5m (5ft).

■ **Flowering season:** winter-growers flower in spring, summer growers and evergreens flower in late summer or early autumn. There is a wide range of colours.

■ **Care:** evergreens need moisture year-round while the others expect it only during their growing season. Plants require little feeding if soil is good but, if desired, can be given complete plant food or slow-release fertiliser when growth begins.

■ **In pots:** the smaller species make good container plants and in cold climates it is the only way to grow species from the winter-rainfall areas. Grow in a greenhouse kept frost-free at night in autumn and winter, and raise temperature to at least 10°C (50°F) during the day. Dry out pots after blooming, remove corms and store clean and dry over summer. In gardens, lift, separate and replant both winter-dormant and summer-dormant species every three years.

Left, bottom: Veltheimias make attractive plants in groups and tolerate shady, dry conditions.

Above, left: Watsonias are attractive plants in garden beds, especially combined with other flowers as here.

Above: Winter-growing Watsonia meriana *produces its rosy-pink flowers mid to late spring. Varieties can be dwarf or tall.*

Zantedeschia

Arum lily, Calla lily

Family: *Araceae (Arum family).*
Type: *rhizome.* **Native to:** *Angola, Zambia and South Africa. All but one species from the summer-rainfall areas; the climate is warm to hot year-round. Rain falls in every month but summers are much wetter than winters. Frosts of -10˚C (14˚F) are possible in parts but not common or prolonged.*

■ **Preferred climate:** cold, cool, frost-free and tropical gardens. Most species are summer-growing/winter dormant and are hardy to at least -12˚C (10˚F). Where winter temperatures fall lower than this, the rhizomes can be lifted in autumn and stored at above freezing until the following spring.

Wurmbea

Family: *Colchicaceae (Colchicum family).* **Type:** *bulb.* **Native to:** *tropical and southern Africa and Western Australia where the climate varies. In the west and south-west of South Africa and in Western Australia, the climate is Mediterranean with wet, frost-free or near frost-free winters and hot, relatively dry summers. In eastern South Africa and in tropical Africa, most rain falls in summer; the fairly dry winters are mild.*

■ **Preferred climate:** near frost-free, frost-free and subtropical gardens. Plants are intolerant of all but the lightest frosts. In colder climates they can be grown in pots that are given the protection of a frost-free greenhouse. In cold-climate gardens, species which are winter-dormant can be planted outside in spring and lifted in autumn.

■ **Planting tips:** most species are planted in autumn. Only those few from the summer-rainfall areas are planted in early spring. Plant bulbs 3cm (1in) deep, about 10cm (4in) apart in fertile, free-draining soil. Full sun is usually the best aspect, except for the summer growers which will thrive in partial shade. Site where they can be left undisturbed.

■ **Growing season:** autumn, winter and early spring, or spring and summer. Ultimate height varies, depending on the species, from 10cm (4in) to 40cm (16in).

■ **Flowering season:** winter-growers flower in late winter and early spring; summer-growers in late summer. The flowers are curious and can have a pleasant, spicy or sweet fragrance.

■ **Care:** keep well watered during the growing season and very lightly moist once dormant. Don't lift bulbs unnecessarily.

■ **In pots:** possibly the best way to grow these plants, whatever your climate. Where winters are more than lightly frosty, grow in a greenhouse kept frost-free at night and at least 10˚C (50˚F) during the day. Winter days can be around 20˚C (68˚F) in their homelands. Leave dormant bulbs in their pots and keep very lightly moist until growth resumes in autumn.

■ **Planting tips:** plant in early spring, 10cm (4in) deep and 30cm (12in) or more apart into moist soil containing rotted organic matter. All species will tolerate waterlogging for short periods (except when dormant) and thrive in sun or shade, but won't flower well in full shade. *Zantedeschia aethiopica* spreads rapidly along the sides of streams or in marshy ground and should not be planted where there is any danger of escape into natural bushland. It is a prohibited noxious weed in some parts of Australia and could be a danger in the southern USA.

■ **Growing season:** spring, summer and early autumn or, in the case of *Z. aethiopica*, the plant is evergreen. Plants grow up to 1.8m (6ft) in height.

■ **Flowering season:** during spring and summer, appearing over a very long period. They may be white, yellow, pink or orange.

■ **Care:** give winter-dormant species plenty of water from the time growth begins and especially through summer. They can not be overwatered. Ease back in autumn then stop entirely. Apply slow-release fertiliser or complete plant food at the beginning of the growing season. In cold climates, lift rhizomes before frost and store dry over winter.

■ **In pots:** beautiful in pots, especially the smaller growing and colourful hybrids of *Z. rehmannii*. In cold climates these can be over-wintered dry in their containers.

Left, top: South Africa's curious Wurmbea spicata *flowers from late winter and has a pleasant fragrance.*

*Below, from left: the shapely flowers and lush foliage of Zantedeschias; Z. rehmannii **has** pink, red or white flowers; 'Green Goddess' is a popular hybrid of Z. aethiopica.*

Bulbs to Plant in
Late Autumn/Winter

Bulbs in this section are planted either towards the end of autumn or in winter. Some may be planted at other times, depending on your climate. If so, this is noted in the "Planting tips" section of individual entries.

All plant dimensions and planting depths are given in metric and imperial measurements. The conversions have been rounded off to the nearest whole number.

Pierre Pilloud·Auscape·Jacana / Andrzej Stachurski·Horizon / Geoffrey Burnie / Jack Hobbs

Anemone

Windflower

Family: *Ranunculaceae (Ranunculus family).* **Type:** *tuber or rhizome.* **Native to:** *temperate regions of Europe, the Middle East and Asia where the climate varies enormously. Bulbous species generally experience a Mediterranean climate with cool to cold winters that are rainy or snowy, followed by warm to hot, relatively dry summers. Climates that are cool and rainy year-round are also included.*

■ **Preferred climate:** cold, cool and frost-free gardens, depending on the species. Some are hardy to -34°C (-30°F), while others prefer warmer, near frost-free winters.

■ **Planting tips:** mid to late autumn (the earlier time in cooler climates) in friable, fertile, well-drained soil. Plant 5cm (2in) deep and about 15cm (6in) apart. Species native to woodlands appreciate dappled shade but the popular poppy Anemone (*Anemone coronaria*) accepts full sun.

■ **Growing season:** in winter and spring. Ultimate height varies, depending on the species, from 8cm (3in) to over 30cm (12in).

■ **Flowering season:** early spring. There is a big range of colours in this genus.

■ **Care:** keep moist while growing but allow to dry after bloom.

■ **In pots:** all species can be grown in containers, the low-growing types shown being especially lovely wth other small, spring flowers.

Babiana

Baboon flower

Family: *Iridaceae (Iris family).*
Type: *corm.* **Native to:** *southern Africa where the winters are mild and wet, the summers dry and warm to hot.*

■ **Preferred climate:** warm areas, especially those with a Mediterranean climate. Will tolerate some summer rain if drainage is sharp. Where summers are very wet, lift bulbs after foliage yellows in spring, then store warm and dry; replant in autumn. Bulbs are safe in the ground where winter temperatures fall to -5°C (23°F). While they may survive much lower temperatures if planted in a sunny, sheltered spot and mulched heavily, Babiana are not recommended for garden use in cold climates.

■ **Planting tips:** plant in mid-autumn, 15-25cm (6-10in) deep – the cooler your climate, the deeper you should plant – in any fertile, free-draining soil. Plants prefer full sun but will accept very light shade. Where winter temperatures fall below -5°C (23°F), plant in early spring. Site where corms can be left undisturbed for years.

■ **Growing season:** in winter and spring to 20-45cm (8-18in), depending on the species.

■ **Flowering season:** in late winter to mid-spring – the earlier time in warm climates – in red, blue, mauve, yellow, cream, white and bi-colours. Some species are fragrant.

■ **Care:** little needed other than moisture during winter and the spring growing season. Clumps may be fed with complete plant food when growth begins.

■ **In pots:** lovely in pots. Use a very well-drained potting mix and feed plants frequently with liquid or soluble fertiliser when in growth. In cold climates, potted, greenhouse-grown Babiana can bloom in winter.

Far left: The Greek windflower, Anemone blanda, *is able to take complete dryness in summer.*

Left: The wood Anemone, A. nemorosa, *makes a lovely ground cover.*

Above, top: Babiana pulchra *produces its impressive, vivid, violet flowers in mid-spring.*

Above: The wine cup Babiana, B. rubrocyanea, *is one of the most striking species.*

Crocosmia

Falling stars, Montbretia

Family: *Iridaceae (Iris family).*
Type: *corm.* **Native to:** *eastern South Africa where the climate is mild to warm year-round with most rain falling in summer.*

■ **Preferred climate:** subtropical, frost-free and cooler areas where temperatures don't fall below -10°C (14°F).

■ **Planting tips:** plant in autumn or winter or, in cooler areas, early spring, in any fertile, well-drained garden soil. Corms should be planted 5-8cm (2-3in) deep in a sunny or partially shady spot. *Crocosmia crocosmiiflora* is extremely invasive. Some of its named hybrids, such as 'Emily McKenzie' and the species with exquisite orange-red flowers, *C. masonorum*, are much less vigorous. *C. masonorum* is not hardy and should be lifted in autumn where winters are always frosty.

■ **Growing season:** spring, summer and early autumn to about 90cm (3ft) tall.

■ **Flowering season:** late summer in shades of red, orange or yellow.

■ **Care:** give plenty of water from the time shoots appear until after blooming; once established, all species can withstand considerable neglect. Where winters are frosty but not severe, mulch bulbs heavily after leaves have died down. In very cold places, lift and store bulbs above freezing until frosts have finished.

■ **In pots:** easily grown in pots, and this is the safest way to enjoy the invasive *C. crocosmiiflora*.

Left, from top: Crocosmia 'Citronella' is a fine yellow hybrid; 'Emily McKenzie' is not as rampant and has striking orange flowers; 'Emberglow' is vibrant and tall, easily reaching 90cm (3ft).

Eucomis

Pineapple lily

Family: *Liliaceae (Lily family)*.
Type: *bulb*. **Native to:** *mostly eastern South Africa: one species in the winter-rainfall south-western area of that country and one in tropical Africa. The climate is warm, frost-free or light frosts only. Rain all year but most falls during the warmer months.*

■ **Preferred climate:** outdoors anywhere with a frost-free growing season of at least five months or a heated greenhouse in colder climates. Plants will tolerate cold snaps down to -10˚C (14˚F), but not deep freezes or months of near-freezing temperatures.

■ **Planting tips:** plant in autumn or winter with their necks above ground level in good-quality, fertile, well-drained soil. Full sun is desirable but plants will tolerate some shade during the day, especially in hot, sunny climates.

■ **Growing season:** spring, summer and early autumn. Sizes vary with species but the biggest ones grow to about 90cm (3ft) tall and half as wide. The species *Eucomis regia* from the south-west of South Africa grows and flowers during winter, dying back by early summer.

■ **Flowering season:** in summer. Spikes are long-lasting and individual flowers may be white with green tinges or yellow-green, and are sometimes darkly outlined.

■ **Care:** keep moist during the growing season. Dormant bulbs can tolerate moderate winter rain if drainage is good. Where rain is heavy and persistent in winter and drainage poor, bulbs will rot. Apply a ration of complete plant food in spring or mulch at this time with compost or rotted manure. Lift and separate bulbs in winter only if necessary. Eucomis does not enjoy frequent disturbance.

■ **In pots:** good in groups in fairly big pots. Store pots out of sight in a dark, airy place over winter.

Above: The exotic, green-tinged flowers of Eucomis comosa *are pleasantly scented.*

Hippeastrum

Amaryllis

Family: *Amaryllidaceae
(Hippeastrum family).* **Type:** *bulb.*
Native to: *central America and
tropical and subtropical South
America where the climate is warm
to hot year-round with light frosts
only occurring in highland areas or
inland at the cooler limit of the
range. Rainfall in this extensive
area varies from year-round to dry
in winter. Humidity is generally
high throughout.*

■ **Preferred climate:** tropical,
subtropical and frost-free gardens.
In colder climates, grow in pots
in a heated greenhouse or in
the conservatory, and maintain a

night temperature of 13°C (55°F) and
about 21°C (70°F) during the day. In
gardens, hybrids will tolerate little, if
any, frost. Some species will accept
a few degrees of frost if planted
against a sunny wall and protected
by a covering of straw or fern fronds.

■ **Planting tips:** in warm-climate
gardens plant spring-flowering
species (the typical Hippeastrums)
any time from mid-autumn to early
spring. In cold climates, where they
are grown for winter display, pot in
early autumn. In the garden, plant
with their necks at, or just below,
the surface and about 25cm (10in)
apart. In pots, the top third of the
bulb should be exposed. Species
that flower in summer are planted in

early spring. All Hippeastrums
demand good drainage and enjoy a
nutritious soil – that is, high in rotted
organic matter. In gardens, leave
undisturbed to slowly increase, and
site in full sun or with a few hours of
dappled midday to afternoon shade.

■ **Growing season:** in warm-
climate gardens, the typical
Hippeastrum grows from spring to
autumn, its leaves appearing with,
or just after, the spring flowers.
Where winters are frost-free with
regular rain, they may be evergreen.
In cold climates, water is reduced
towards the end of summer and
withheld for the first two months of
autumn to force the bulbs into
dormancy. They are then re-started

into growth with heat and water to flower for winter. The strappy leaves of Hippeastrums are about 45cm (18in) long; the flowers rise to a height of about 60cm (2ft).

■ **Flowering season:** early spring in gardens or winter in cool climates, if forced. Flowers may be white, pink, orange or red with many combinations of these. Natural species often have smaller, more elegant flowers than do hybrids.

■ **Care:** keep lightly moist when flower buds first appear, gradually giving more water as growth proceeds. Apply a ration of complete plant food when leaf growth begins or feed plants monthly, from mid-spring to mid-summer, with liquid organic fertiliser. Remove faded flowers. In warm-climate gardens, Hippeastrums flower better if they can be kept dry in winter.

■ **In pots:** keep lightly moist after potting, then increase water and start to feed as the flower bud rises. Keep moist but not sodden during summer and feed lightly but frequently with liquid organic fertiliser or apply slow-release granules when growth begins. Dry off by the end of summer (or mid-autumn in warm climates) and keep dry for at least two months. This is important in cold climates but less so in warm-climate gardens.

*Above, from left: Hippeastrum papillio **is a beautifully patterned, relatively unknown species; red, eye-catching Hippeastrums;** 'Germa' is a **wonderfully elegant hybrid seen mostly in Britain.***

Lilium

Lily

Family: *Liliaceae (Lily family).*
Type: *bulb.* **Native to:** *Europe, Asia and North America, mostly within the temperate latitudes. The climate there varies widely but winters can be cold, cool or, less commonly, frost-free. Most lilies come from places where rain or snow falls year-round but there are also some from Mediterranean climates that experience relatively dry summers.*

■ **Preferred climate:** cold, cool and frost-free gardens. Liliums are plants of the northern hemisphere temperate zone and, with the exception of *Lilium longiflorum*, are not well suited to lowland subtropical or tropical climates.

■ **Planting tips:** plant in autumn and winter about 20cm (8in) deep, except for *L. candidum*, the top of which should be at soil level. Space 20-25cm (8-10in) apart and plant in very rich soil that drains freely yet stays moist. Lilies must have moisture at all times but cannot sit in sodden soil. They thrive where

their roots are shaded and cool but their leaves can reach the sun. Generally, they prefer acidic soils but there are some which will tolerate alkaline conditions. In cold climates, lilies are more usually planted in early spring.

■ **Growing season:** Winter (in warm climates), spring, summer and early autumn up to 1.5m (5ft) tall.

■ **Flowering season:** late spring and summer in a huge range of colours and patterns.

■ **Care:** never let the bulbs dry out even when dormant, but don't saturate them in winter. When growth begins, start to water regularly, giving more water as plants grow and summer approaches. After blooming, less water helps the bulbs mature. Apply complete plant food or slow-release fertiliser when growth appears and feed once or twice more before flowering with liquid or soluble plant food. When plants die back, mulch them with leaf mould or compost. When cutting flowers,

leave at least a third of the stem or the plant will not be able to feed itself.

■ **In pots:** lower-growing species make wonderful pot subjects and can be planted more closely together than in the garden. Grow them outside but bring indoors when they are in bloom.

Below, left: America's easily grown leopard lily, Lilium pardalinum, **has fragrant, exotic flowers and can tolerate wetter soil.**

Below: Strongly fragrant L. longiflorum **is one of the few species that suits frost-free and subtropical gardens.**

Right, top: 'Golden Clarion' is a trumpet hybrid with lovely, clear yellow flowers.

Right, bottom: Lily breeders have produced hundreds of big, showy hybrids. This one is 'Empress of India'.

Pamianthe

Family: *Amaryllidaceae*
(Hippeastrum family). **Type:** *bulb.*
Native to: *Peru where the climate is*
warm to hot year-round. Rain falls
in every month but late autumn
and winter is the driest period.
Frosts are unknown.

■ **Preferred climate:** frost-free,
subtropical and tropical gardens.
Plants will not accept frosts. In
colder climates, grow in pots in a
greenhouse kept at 10˚C (50˚F), or
above in winter.

■ **Planting tips:** plant
mid-autumn to mid-winter 10cm (4in)
deep, 38cm (15in) apart in deep,
moist soil that contains rotted
organic matter. A warm, bright but
shady position is essential, such as
against a sunny wall but shaded by
shrubs or overhanging tree branches.

■ **Growing season:** year-round;
least active during late autumn and
early winter. Plants grow to a height
of about 60cm (2ft).

■ **Flowering season:** mid to late
summer or early autumn. The big,
cream-coloured flowers are fragrant.

■ **Care:** keep very lightly moist
from mid-autumn to late winter.
When new growth begins, gradually
increase water, giving the maximum
amounts during the latter part of
spring and in summer. After
blooming, taper off the watering. Feed
monthly with liquid or soluble plant
food from early spring to flowering.
Control mealy bugs, thrips and mites
at first sign of infestation.

■ **In pots:** Pamianthe make
striking and unusual pot plants that
can fill a room with fragrance when

in bloom. Grow three bulbs in a
large tub of quality potting mix into
which has been blended a ration of
complete plant food or slow-release
fertiliser. Plant bulbs with their
necks at soil level. In cold climates,
maintain a minimum night
temperature of 10˚C (50˚F), rising
to 15˚C (59˚F) during the day in
winter. Raise temperatures in line
with the seasons so that, in summer,
night temperatures are kept at
18-20˚C (64-68˚F), day temperatures
at 27˚C (80˚F).

Above: Fragrant and shapely,
Pamianthe peruviana **is an**
unusual bulb that is ideal for
humid, rainy, frost-free areas.

Stenomesson

Family: *Amaryllidaceae (Hippeastrum family).* **Type:** *bulb.*
Native to: *Andes mountains of Peru, Bolivia and Ecuador at altitudes of up to 3000m (10,000ft). The climate there is mild to hot year-round, depending on the altitude and basically frost-free, except at the higher elevations where light frosts are possible. Rain falls in every month, but autumn and winter are the driest seasons.*

■ **Preferred climate:** frost-free, subtropical and highland tropical gardens. In colder climates, grow in a greenhouse kept above 7°C (45°F) in autumn and winter.

■ **Planting tips:** plant in late autumn with the tops of the bulbs just above soil level and spaced about 30cm (12in) apart. Soil should be well drained and contain plenty of rotted organic matter. Plant in full sun or partial shade.

■ **Growing season:** spring and summer to about 38cm (15in) in height. The grey-green leaves are strappy.

■ **Flowering season:** mid-spring to early summer, the orange, pendulous bells appearing in a cluster atop leafless stems.

■ **Care:** in frost-free climates, the plant may be evergreen, in which case it needs some moisture year-round but keep just damp in autumn and winter. In cooler areas it dies back completely in autumn. Give minimal water at this time. Feed plants with complete plant food or liquid or soluble fertiliser when growth begins. In cold climates potted plants need greenhouse protection with a winter minimum of 7°C (45°F).

Right: Grow tender, elegantly shaped Stenomesson miniatum in a frost-free garden or heated greenhouse.

Index